A Worrier's Guide to the Bible

50 Verses to Ease Anxieties

GARY ZIMAK

Liguori
LIGUORI, MISSOURI

Imprimi Potest:
Harry Grile, CSsR, Provincial
Denver Province, The Redemptorists

Published by Liguori Publications
Liguori, Missouri 63057

To order, call 800-325-9521, or visit liguori.org.

Library of Congress Cataloging-in-Publication Data

Zimak, Gary.
 A worrier's guide to the Bible / Gary Zimak.—1st ed.
    p. cm.
1. Christian life—Catholic authors. 2. Worry—Religious aspects—Catholic
Church. 3. Worry—Biblical teaching. I. Title.
 BX2350.3.Z56 2012
 248.8'6—dc23
                                                                2012018148

p ISBN 978-0-7648-2163-9
e ISBN 978-0-7648-6728-6

Liguori Publications, a nonprofit corporation, is an apostolate of The Redemptorists. To learn more about The Redemptorists, visit Redemptorists.com.

Printed in the United States of America
16 15 14 13 12 / 5 4 3 2
First Edition

CONTENTS

Acknowledgments

To my wonderful wife and best friend, Eileen, thank you for making my life a complete joy. Without your support of my work and constant dedication to the needs of our family, this book would not have been possible. Thank you, Honey…I love you!

To my twin daughters, Mary and Elizabeth, I am so blessed to be your dad. Thanks for always being so excited about my work and for living your Catholic faith….I love you, girls!

To my mom and dad, Gerry and Ed Zimak, thank you for your constant love and for having me baptized into the Catholic faith as an infant. You taught me what it meant to sacrifice for your family, and I'm grateful for that lesson.

To my late mother-in-law, Betty Moynahan, thank you for teaching me the about the importance of eucharistic adoration and for sharing your love of the Catholic faith. Your passing left a void in my life, but I still feel your presence each day.

Finally, I'd like to acknowledge my Blessed Mother, Mary. On October 7, 2011, I formally consecrated my life to Jesus through Mary. My life has changed dramatically since that day and, with your help, I have become closer to your Son than I ever thought possible. Thank you, Mother!

I'm grateful to all of you and to the countless others who made this book possible. Without all of your love and support, this work would never have come to fruition.

Foreword

I knew Gary's first book would be a solid, popular resource for Catholics for several reasons. The first indication came following one of Gary's apologetics segments on my radio program. (Gary is a frequent guest on my daily syndicated talk show *Catholic Connection With Teresa Tomeo*.)

After Gary received the go-ahead for *A Worrier's Guide to the Bible* from Liguori Publications, he asked if he might mention the book and its then-pending release date during our interview. Now there is an old saying out there reminding us if we want someone to remember what we say we need to say it at least seven times. Well, Gary and I did our best to follow that sound suggestion. We told my listeners when the book would be published. We repeatedly directed them to his website, which had details front-and-center on his home page. Between the two of us we mentioned the release date at least seven times, if not more. However, despite our best efforts, after the interview I was flooded with e-mails and phone calls asking for the book's title and how to purchase it as well. The comments were another clue that *A Worrier's Guide to the Bible* would be a hit. I don't think there was one listener who didn't explain by voice mail or e-mail why he or she needed this book. Some spoke of family concerns. Others commented on their economic situations. Others expressed a general concern for worrying less and trusting God more. I had visions of these folks with cash or credit card in hand ready and willing to buy the book and as quickly as possible.

In addition to the reaction from my radio listeners is the reaction from the people I meet in my work as a motivational speaker who give me more reason to believe this book will pack a powerful punch with the public. Despite what Scripture teaches us, people still have issues they worry about. There are the parents I meet who are concerned about protecting their children from the ravages of a culture that is for the most part morally bankrupt. There are the teens who tell me they fret over their self image and struggle with eating disorders, peer pressure, and bullying. There are the men who say they are losing sleep because of concerns connected to providing for the family in an increasingly insecure economy. There is the long line of ladies I meet at women's conferences around the country who wait to tell me how they continually struggle in their attempts to measure up to a seemingly never-ending list of societal pressures and demands that call for them to have it all and do it all while being everything to every person in their lives. In other words, as a good deacon friend of mine always says, "*everybody's got something.*" The worrywart in us regularly rears its ugly head even though the Lord keeps telling us through the Word to trust that God has the answers. The most frequent words of wisdom given to us from Jesus in the New Testament have to do with fear and worry. As a matter of fact, I have heard many a priest and preacher say that the phrase "do not be afraid," or some version of it, appears in Scripture 365 times, equal to the number of days in a year. Despite the fact that the Lord keeps telling us to "let go, let God," we still worry.

That's why this book is so important. We can tell ourselves not to worry, but it is still going to happen. We are human. If we are still on this planet, the Lord is not through with us yet. God has work for us to do, and much of that work for most of us ties in with our own purification and perfection. *A Worrier's Guide to the Bible* doesn't make false promises. It doesn't lead the reader to believe that by picking up this book all their anxieties, fears, and worries will melt away like butter on a pile of steaming-hot mashed potatoes. What it does do is provide a place to go when we feel the fear start creeping in again. In a practical and helpful approach, it takes a look at subjects that every Christian can identify with: confusion, fear, doubt, trials, and sickness, just to name a few. *A Worrier's Guide to the Bible* won't solve all of our problems, but it will help us deal with them better—and from a truly Christian and scriptural perspective.

What I also greatly appreciate about *A Worrier's Guide to the Bible* is its very personal touch. Some of the best advice I was ever given is that writers should write what they know. Gary, as he explains, is no stranger to worry, and he writes about his own challenges in this beautiful book straight from his heart.

Finally, while there have been many books written on apologetics, defending and explaining various doctrines and beliefs, I don't know of any book that tackles a topic so timely and familiar to so many of us.

This book is a keeper; one to keep on the nightstand or on the kitchen table, close enough to grab when we need that daily dose of knowing that God is nearer than we think.

Teresa Tomeo
Nationally Syndicated Radio Host
Best-Selling Catholic Author
Motivational Speaker
www.TeresaTomeo.com

Introduction

(From One Worrier to Another)

If you're reading this, it's very likely that you and I have something in common: a tendency to worry. Furthermore, I'll go out on a limb and state that, over the course of my life, I've probably worried about as many (if not more) issues than any of you. Why do I feel the need to share this information? Wouldn't it help my credibility to assure you that I've always trusted God's plan and never worried about anything? In reality, when it comes to anxiety, I believe in the expression *it takes one to know one*. I have been a chronic worrier for most of my life, and I know how stressful it can be. Fortunately, I can also tell you that there is a silver lining to this apparent cloud that often goes unnoticed. Over the course of my life as a worrier, I've learned an important lesson: *Anxiety can be a blessing.*

Before you think I've lost my mind, let me give you some additional details that will hopefully clarify my position. I started worrying at a very young age. When I was in the second grade, the father of one of my classmates passed away suddenly. I immediately started worrying that my own father would die. After that came fears that my mother would die, that I would die (I "suffered" from every fatal disease imaginable!), that I would be made fun of or get beat up in school, that my irritable bowel syndrome would flare up in the classroom, etc.

Do you get the picture? Well, *you ain't seen nothin' yet*...I haven't even gotten to my life after grammar school! In my high school years, such issues as acne, shyness, dating ineptness, and lack of direction about my future were added to the mix. My college years provided many additional opportunities for worry, but also an unexpected revelation. One day, as I was walking on the campus of Drexel University, I was handed a little green book by a member of the Gideons. If you're familiar with that organization, you're probably aware that the book was a miniature New Testament. Having always been a religious person (although not possessing a strong knowledge of my Catholic faith), I opened that Bible and was struck by something I saw.

Thumbing through the first couple of pages, I noticed the heading, *"Where To Find Help When...,"* followed by a number of familiar emotions (fear, anxiety, depression, discouragement, worry, etc.) along with a suggested Bible verse for each. I began to look up the verses that were recommended for my many anxieties and experienced an unfamiliar sensation. For the first time in my life I found myself being comforted by the words of the Bible. I kept that copy of the New Testament in a safe place and referred to that list and the corresponding verses many times throughout my college years and beyond. It became my source of peace whenever I encountered a stressful situation in my life.

Let's get back to my statement that anxiety can be a blessing. If it wasn't for all of my fears, I may never have turned to God for help. As I learned when I opened up that little green book, the Lord is waiting to speak words of comfort to us through the pages of sacred Scripture. Whenever we are faced with problems in our lives, we have two opposing choices: we can either worry or we can turn to God. The Lord does not want us to worry and can help us to find peace, even as we're being pounded by the storms in our lives.

Most of us are aware that the Bible contains many passages urging trust instead of worry. Unfortunately, we often have difficulty finding these verses when we need them. That, my friends, is why I wrote this book. You hold in your hands a "weapon" to use whenever you are tempted to begin worrying. It is a road map that you can use to guide you to peace, even in the midst of chaos. You can read sequentially, choose a random verse, or concentrate on your "favorite" anxiety-prone situation. Each Bible verse is supplemented with some words of insight, calling on the fullness of Catholic theology in order to better fortify your "anti-anxiety" arsenal. As you read the passages and meditations contained in these pages, it is my belief that you will begin to experience the peace that only God can provide.

In order to obtain the maximum benefit from this book, I recommend that you take it to an adoration chapel or church and read it in the presence of the Blessed Sacrament. By doing so, you will be able to hear the Lord speak to you in a most profound way. If you encounter a verse that particularly touches you, I encourage you to open the Bible and explore it in greater detail.

Comfort in God's Word

It is not that once you learn the value of using the Bible as a weapon against anxiety you'll never worry again. Realistically, many of us will fight this battle for the rest of our lives. However, there is a much better chance of finding comfort in our lives by opening up the Bible than if we just leave it on the shelf.

As I write this, I'm dealing with two significant issues in my life. At my day job, we are on the verge of what could be a major layoff. Although it's always been my dream to pursue Catholic apologetics on a full-time basis, I'd prefer to do it on my terms. As I need to support my family, a sudden job loss is not something that excites me.

On the other hand, the Lord may be viewing this as the push I need to embark on a new and fruitful adventure. As I pore over and meditate upon the verses included in this book, however, I'm discovering something very interesting. Through the pages of the Bible, the Lord is reassuring me that worry is useless. Every time I start to feel anxious, I run across another verse that calms my fears. As long as I'm praying and reading God's message in the Bible, I find it very difficult to worry.

Aside from the prospect of being unemployed, I mentioned another potential source of anxiety in my life. Would you like to know what it is? You may find this amusing, but I've been concerned that I wouldn't be able to complete this book on time. I even joked with my wife that I'm so stressed out and anxious that I need to finish my book...just so I can read it! *As you've probably deduced, the fact that you're reading this serves as proof that any time I spent worrying was wasted.* In closing, I'd like to leave all of you with a powerful message from Saint Padre Pio of Pietrelcina. It is a five-word summary of all that I'm hoping to accomplish with this book..."*Pray, hope, and don't worry!*"

Through the intercession of Saint Padre Pio, may we all learn to use our time *productively* and always turn to the Lord in times of need.

God bless you!

GARY ZIMAK

CHAPTER 1

Confusion

Over the course of our lives, we are faced with situations that require us to make decisions. While some decisions are more important than others, they all share one thing in common: The choices we make have an effect on our lives.

Should I take this new job?
Should I buy a new car?
Should I become a priest/sister?
Should I relocate to a new area?
Should I let my kids go away to college?
Should I break off this relationship?

As Christians, we want (or at least we *should* want) to do the right thing at all times. In other words, we should desire to do God's will. Therefore, before making any serious decision, we should ask ourselves the question: *What would God want me to do?*

While that sounds good, it is often easier said than done. Determining the Lord's will for our lives is sometimes difficult and can be a confusing process. This confusion will often lead us to worry. We can take comfort in the fact that the Lord is standing by and ready to help us understand God's will for our lives.

The Bible is filled with stories of ordinary people being chosen to accomplish some very extraordinary tasks. In each of these cases, the Lord provides the necessary guidance. While it may require work on our part (prayer, meditation, spiritual reading, visiting Jesus in the Blessed Sacrament), God will never leave us stranded. However, it's also important to remember that although the Lord will help us to know *what* to do, God may not explain *why* we should do it. In these cases, we simply have to trust in the Lord. The important lesson for us is that we should always turn to the Lord in times of confusion. The following verses and corresponding reflections remind us of this opportune choice.

1.

"Now go, I will assist you in speaking and teach you what you are to say" (Exodus 4:12).

One of the most common but costly mistakes we commit when trying to make a decision is neglecting to ask for the Lord's help. We spend much of our time examining options and trying to make the perfect choice. This confusion eventually turns to panic and we feel almost frozen. We obtain information from friends and people who may be more experienced than ourselves and often we are more confused than when we started. Most of us are all too familiar with what it's like to spend a sleepless night, tossing and turning while we ponder a myriad of unacceptable alternatives. Is life really supposed to be *this* difficult?

Moses felt he was unqualified to lead the Israelites out of slavery in Egypt, so he asked the Lord to reconsider. Reminding God of his lack of speaking skills, the reluctant leader pressured the Lord to choose someone more qualified. Amazingly, even after God promised to give him the words, Moses remained adamant about his lack of qualifications. In an example of amazing patience, the Lord proposed that Aaron, Moses' brother and an eloquent speaker, could act as Moses' spokesman. Finally, Moses accepted his mission.

What was Moses' main problem? He ignored the Lord's offer of assistance and thought that he would have to do everything himself. He somehow managed to disregard the fact that the Lord promised not only to assist him but to actually give him the words. When we struggle to make a decision without asking for the Lord's help, aren't we actually doing the same thing? Many of us like to be in control and, as a result, completely take God out of the picture. We are determined to solve our problems by ourselves, and when we run into trouble and become confused, we worry. The cause of this is often due to our excessive pride or lack of faith. Although it's not easy to admit, we sometimes feel weak when we have to ask for the Lord's help or don't really think that he will help us. Instead, we'll spend the night tossing and turning, worrying about what to do. Does this make a lot of sense?

If you are struggling to make a decision and want to make the right choice, do you really believe that God will not assist you? The Lord is always with us, but we need to ask and listen. How do I reach out to my children who no longer attend Mass? What is the best response when people attack the Church? Should I take a new job that requires me to relocate? When facing a challenge in your life, turn to the Lord for help. Ask God what you should do. While it's highly unlikely that you are going to hear him speak to you out loud, you will be able to *hear* the Lord's answer in the silence of your heart. If something is in accordance with God's will, you'll often experience a feeling of peace and contentment.

The Lord knows that, just like Moses, we can be stubborn at times. Unfortunately, by refusing to rely on God's help, we prolong our agony and run the risk of making poor decisions. If we turn to the Lord for guidance, we'll not only experience peace, but we can be sure we're following his will for our lives. What could be better than that?

Lord, help me to remember that you are always there to help me when I am confused. Give me the grace to relinquish control and be willing to ask for (and accept) your direction. Amen.

2.

"By faith Abraham obeyed when he was called to go out to a place that he was to receive as an inheritance; he went out, not knowing where he was to go" (Hebrews 11:8).

Life is always easier when we know what to expect. Even though we never know what will happen for certain, we like to have an idea of what lies in store for us. Unexpected emergencies and crises can really become an occasion to panic. Even bad weather can be enough to put us in a foul mood or cause moderate to severe grumbling. Personally, I like to know what's ahead for me each day. Unfortunately, life doesn't work that way. As we travel life's highway, there are many twists and turns along the way. God allows things to happen in our lives in order to help us achieve our salvation. Our response to these events can make a big difference in where we end up after our earthly life is over.

As Christians, we have much in common with Abraham. We are all called by Almighty God to travel an unknown road that can lead us to our promised inheritance. Of course, that unknown road is known as *life* and the inheritance is *heaven*. Just like Abraham, we are invited to set out and follow the Lord, not knowing all of the details. How do we respond? Do we respond with faithful acceptance (like Abraham) or do we complain about uncertainties and inconveniences?

Promised numerous descendants by the Lord, Abraham had no children and a wife who was elderly. Still, he trusted that God's word was trustworthy. When Sarah miraculously conceived and bore a son (Isaac), Abraham was asked to sacrifice that son (Genesis 22:1–19). Talk about a leap of faith!

How do we react when asked by the Lord to carry an unexpected cross such as illness, unemployment or the death of a loved one? Often we get upset declaring, *it's too confusing*! *I don't know what I'm going to do! I need more information!* Abraham obeyed the Lord's commands without knowing the fullness of God's design. That is the meaning of faith. If all of the facts are known, faith becomes irrelevant. Can we honestly say that we trust the Lord as much as Abraham did?

Although we should always be willing to trust God even when we don't have all of the answers, there is nothing wrong with asking the Lord to help us understand the confusing events in our lives. *Why did I lose my job? Why did my father die? Why is it so difficult for me to trust?*

These are all valid questions and can be directed to the Lord. The Lord accompanies us and desires to calm our fears. Sometimes, God will even provide concrete reasons for the struggle, but not always. Over the course of my life, I have received some surprising answers to my questions. There were other times that I did not receive answers. I've learned to view these occasions as opportunities to express my love for the Lord by trusting, even when I don't understand the way forward.

Due to the fact that we are human, confusion will always be a part of our lives. Things will happen that just "don't make sense." It is impossible to understand everything that God does (Isaiah 55:8–9), and accepting this will bring us deep peace.

> *I realize that I'm a "fair weather" Christian at times, Jesus, and I need your help. Give me the strength to trust in you even when I don't know why things are happening in my life. Amen.*

3.

"Jesus spoke to them again, saying, 'I am the light of the world. Whoever follows me will never walk in darkness, but will have the light of life'" (John 8:12).

Have you ever gotten up in the middle of the night and tried to make your way across the dark bedroom? You proceed with caution, with hands extended, hoping to feel any obstacles before you walk into them. If you're like me, it's the shoes or boxes lying on the floor that trip you up as you unsuccessfully attempt to navigate in the dark. Let's face it, it's a lot easier to walk around when you can see than when you can't. Instead of walking face first into the wall, you can simply walk around it. Rather than doing an unintentional flip over a box on the floor, you can easily step over it.

In a similar way, life is full of darkness. We are surrounded by obstacles and dangers that can tempt us, possibly causing us to fall into sin. Without a *light* to help us navigate the roads of our daily lives, we have the same chance of falling or running into a wall as we do in our darkened bedroom. When we fall by sinning, however, the damage can be a lot worse than a stubbed toe or a bruised arm. It can affect our eternal salvation.

Fortunately there is some good news, or should I say, *Good News*. Jesus Christ is the light that we need to keep us on the right path. His assurance that Christians will not walk in darkness should make us very happy. Once we turn our lives over to the Lord and follow Christ's teachings, we no longer have to stumble through life frightened and confused.

The key point, however, is that we must actively *follow* Jesus. This implies obeying his teachings and not just claiming membership in the Church. Many Catholics today feel that they can pick and choose the Church teachings they follow, disregarding the ones with which they disagree. This phenomenon, known as cafeteria Catholicism, is a dangerous practice that prohibits one from being a true follower of Christ. If we enthrone ourselves as the ultimate authority for deciding moral beliefs, can we possibly say we are followers of Jesus? In fact, instead, we are following ourselves.

How exactly does our Lord reveal his light to us? One very powerful way is through the *Catechism of the Catholic Church*. In this document, we are blessed to have a compilation of two thousand years of Church teaching. Consisting of Bible verses, official Vatican teaching, and commentary by the early Church Fathers and saints, this masterpiece summarizes the teaching of the Catholic Church in a useful and effective way.

Jesus is truly the Light of the World. Remaining close to him will ensure that we don't walk in the darkness. As with any light, however, we need to flip the switch in order for it to shine. Our Lord founded a Church (Matthew 16:18) and helps us find salvation. Through the Church, God provides us with an unending source of light in order to illuminate the darkness and walk treacherous roads through life. We are invited to do our part by flipping the switch and using the light to guide our steps.

Dear Jesus, thank you for being a light in the darkness. Help me to love and follow the teachings of your Church so that I don't stumble on the road that leads to eternal life. Amen.

4.

"Will not God then secure the rights of his chosen ones who call out to him day and night? Will he be slow to answer them?" (Luke 18:7).

Why doesn't God answer me?

Have you ever asked or thought of asking this question? If so, you're not alone. At some point in our lives, we've all been faced with a situation in which God seems unresponsive. It can be especially frustrating when we are trying to make a decision and don't know what to do. We turn to the Lord for advice, praying for an answer to our problem. If you're like me, there have probably been times when you've given up, thinking that God wants you to handle this one on your own. Take it from me that this is not a good idea. While there are times when God says no, we shouldn't assume that the Lord doesn't hear us just because our answer isn't coming fast enough.

Some supporting evidence for this advice can be found in the parable of the Persistent Widow, found in the Gospel of Luke. One thing I like about this parable is that Luke tells us exactly what it means. This removes the guesswork and is perfect for nonbiblical scholars. According to the evangelist, this parable is about the "need to pray always and not to lose heart" (Luke 18:1). Pretty clear, isn't it? God desires our goodness out of love for us, so if we pray for something harmful or sinful (even though we may not consider it so), we might be initially distressed at the will of the Father. But when we sincerely need something, we are encouraged to keep praying for the Lord's answer, which could be in the form of an affirming *yes,* a definite *no,* a gentle reminder to *keep praying and wait,* or simply a *deep peace in the moment.*

In this parable, the dishonest judge finally grants the widow's request, not because he cares about doing the right thing, but because of her persistence. As with most of Jesus' parables, we have to understand the point that Jesus is trying to make and be careful not to get hung up on the details. Christ often uses hyperbole (exaggeration) in order to make a point. In this case, the Lord isn't necessarily trying to compare our relationship with God to that of the woman and the evil judge but is instead trying to make the point that we should be persistent in prayer.

Why did Jesus use such a radical example, involving a judge who granted a woman's request only to get rid of her? First, it got the listeners' attention and also because using a simple example made the parable more understandable. In order to drive the point home, Jesus contrasts God with the dishonest judge. In other words, if this evil man eventually answers the woman's request, imagine how much more the good Lord will answer the prayers of those who love him.

If you're confused and praying to the Lord for direction, don't stop! Even if things in your life are looking bleak and it appears that God is ignoring you, keep asking! This parable reminds us of the need to be persistent in prayer. Why isn't God answering? Maybe it is because the time isn't right, because you still need to learn something, or because God desires you to be persistent in prayer. Until you receive an answer, imitate the persistent widow and *keep on asking!*

Lord, please help me to be patient and have greater trust in your perfect timing. When I'm tempted to stop praying, allow me to recall the story of the persistent widow who never gave up, even when her initial requests went unanswered. Amen.

5.

"Trust in the LORD with all your heart, on your own intelligence do not rely" (Proverbs 3:5).

At first glance, this verse seems to imply that Christians should not think for themselves. If we really trust in the Lord with all our heart, God will make all the decisions for us. Unfortunately (or fortunately, depending on your point of view), that's not what this verse means. In reality, it cautions us against thinking that we're smarter than God.

I am blessed to be an Extraordinary Minister of Holy Communion, and I have the privilege of bringing Jesus to the residents of a local nursing home. A few days ago, a woman approached me asking to receive the Eucharist. I was confused because her name wasn't on our list. I asked her if she was Catholic and confirmed that she was. I gave her Communion and inquired if she was a new resident. She told me that she's been there for a while and proceeded to explain why she wasn't on the *Catholic* list. When her husband died, she became angry at God and stopped receiving holy Communion and wanted nothing to do with the Church. But now, she told me, "I came to my senses."

How many times have you heard a similar story or done this yourself? Something happens in your life such as the death of a spouse, a divorce, the inability to become pregnant, and you begin to wonder why God would allow these things to happen, thus abandoning or pulling away from the Lord. While God understands that doing this is just a means of coping with grief, it is important to remember that the Lord is also our comforter and deliverer, desiring to grace us always, especially in times of great distress.

It's hard to argue that anyone had more things go wrong than Job. To this day, he remains the ultimate example of Murphy's Law[1]. If something could go wrong in his life, it did. Initially Job accepted his sufferings without complaining, but eventually he made the mistake of trying to figure out the tragic happenings in his life. God (not so subtly) put Job on the spot and asked probing questions: "Where were you when I laid the foundation of the earth? Tell me, if you have understanding. Who determined its measurements—surely you know! Or who stretched the line upon it?" (Job 38:4–5).

After several more unanswerable questions from the Lord, Job finally *got it* and repented. We make the same mistake every time we lash out at God or the Church because we don't like or understand something that happens in our lives. In his infinite wisdom, God allows things to happen which we don't understand. One of the best examples of this happened 2,000 years ago on a hill named Calvary. Jesus Christ, the Son of God, was crucified by the very people he came to save. What about this event makes sense? Why would God allow this to happen? What good could possibly result from this barbaric act? Of course, we all know that this senseless act of violence resulted in the salvation of all humankind.

When God allows bad things to happen in our lives, there is always a reason. We may not always be able to understand the reason, but in these precise moments we must trust. Accepting the will of God will bring us great peace.

---

1 An old adage that states: "anything that can go wrong certainly will."

Sometimes we get angry when we don't get our own way, Lord. We think that we know what's best for our lives instead of trusting in you. Please increase our trust and help us to always remember that your wisdom is infinite and your will is perfect. Amen.

6.

"Listen! I am standing at the door knocking; if you hear my voice and open the door, I will come in to you and eat with you, and you with me" (Revelation 3:20, New Revised Standard Version of the Bible).

I often tell the story of how I was baptized into the Catholic faith as an infant, went to Catholic school for twelve years and attended Mass every week, but had no real relationship with the Lord for most of that time. In late 2004, I started experiencing some strange medical symptoms (weight loss, nausea, dizziness) and had to confront my mortality. I made a decision to dedicate the remainder of my life to learning more about the Catholic faith and sharing it with others. Eventually, my symptoms disappeared and no definitive diagnosis was made. My life, however, changed drastically as I finally discovered what it was like to know the Lord. At first, it may appear that Jesus waited until 2004 to knock on my door. In reality, Christ was knocking for several years and was waiting for *me* to open the door.

When faced with a decision or confused about events in our lives, we often forget to ask for the Lord's assistance. As is stated in the above verse from the Book of Revelation, Jesus won't force us to follow. He'll knock and call but is ultimately always waiting for us to open the door. This concept is beautifully illustrated in the painting

Christ at Heart's Door by Warner Sallman. In this familiar piece of artwork, Jesus is depicted knocking at a closed door. The most notable feature of the image is the absence of a doorknob on the outside of the door. The common interpretation of this anomaly is that our Lord is always knocking at the door of our heart, but it must be opened from the inside. Christ will never force his way into our hearts.

When faced with a difficult or confusing problem, what's the first thing we usually do, besides worry? Generally, we'll seek out an expert who can help us make a good decision. Whether we're dealing with car problems, parenting issues, or relationship problems, we try to find someone who's been there, done that. It's sad that, even when faced with critical issues, we often neglect to consult the ultimate expert— Jesus! Because "the Word became flesh and made his dwelling among us" (John 1:14), Jesus knows firsthand what it's like to experience the difficulties of life. While still retaining his divinity, the Lord "emptied himself, taking the form of a slave" (Philippians 2:7) and voluntarily submitted to the inconveniences that go with being human.

Jesus understands what it's like to walk in our shoes and waits patiently to be invited into our hearts and our lives. He is ready to assist us with our difficult decisions and grant us peace in the midst of turmoil. We can encounter him through the pages of the Bible and through prayer, but there is another way in which he is present in the fullest way possible. Jesus waits for us, often ignored and unnoticed, in the tabernacle of every Catholic church and in numerous adoration chapels around the world. The same Lord and Savior who walked the face of the earth 2,000 years ago is waiting silently for us to pay him a visit. While we are there, we can tell him we love him and ask for assistance in dealing with our problems. Jesus is knocking and wants to be a part of your life. Will you open the door and let him in?

....

*Thank you for knocking on the door of my heart, Lord. Please
come in and help me to be a better person. Amen.*

....

7.

**"Then they said to each other, 'Were not our hearts burning [within
us] while he spoke to us on the way and opened the scriptures to us?'"
(Luke 24:32)**

When faced with a difficult problem in our life, wouldn't it be great
if we could call Jesus on his cell phone and ask for advice? It would
take the guesswork out of our tough decisions and provide comfort
in times of uncertainty. Although the Church teaches that the Lord
speaks to us through the Bible, it's often difficult to hear his words or
understand their meaning in the pages of sacred Scripture.

Although every Christian denomination claims to follow the Bible,
there is a great deal of disagreement about biblical interpretation. Let's
face it, the Bible can be confusing at times. Without an authoritative
interpreter, the Bible can become a matter of personal opinion. If one
asked fifty people to read the same passage and explain its meaning,
you could easily end up with fifty different interpretations. In the Acts
of the Apostles, Saint Luke emphasizes the need for an authoritative
interpreter when he tells of the encounter between Philip and the
Ethiopian eunuch:

> *Now there was an Ethiopian eunuch, a court official of the Candace,*
> *that is, the queen of the Ethiopians, in charge of her entire treasury, who*
> *had come to Jerusalem to worship, and was returning home. Seated*
> *in his chariot, he was reading the prophet Isaiah. The Spirit said to*
> *Philip, "Go and join up with that chariot." Philip ran up and heard*
> *him reading Isaiah the prophet and said, "Do you understand what*
> *you are reading?" He replied, "How can I, unless someone instructs*
> *me?" So he invited Philip to get in and sit with him.*

ACTS 8:27–31

Another example can be found in Saint Luke's account of the two travelers on the road to Emmaus. They were joined by a very special tutor who helped them to understand the Scriptures: "Then beginning with Moses and all the prophets, he interpreted to them what referred to him in all the scriptures" (Luke 24:27). The tutor, Jesus, was not recognized by these travelers until the breaking of the bread (Luke 24:30) opened their eyes. After the Lord vanished, they expressed their frustration at failing to recognize him.

In the biblical account of the journey to Emmaus, only one of the travelers is named (Cleopas). Although not spelled out in the Bible, the other pilgrim also has a name. Depending on the situation, that name is Gary or Joe or Cheryl or Eileen, etc. Many times *we* are that other individual, not realizing that Jesus is right beside us helping us to understand the Bible. How? Through the teaching office (the magisterium) of the Catholic Church. While not offering a line-by-line interpretation, the Church gives us a framework that helps us better comprehend the meaning of the Bible.

The Church encourages us to read the Bible frequently. For in the pages of sacred Scripture we hear the Lord speaking directly to us. However, the Bible should not be read in a vacuum. Understanding Church doctrine will help to make sense out of what could be a confusing book and prevent us from possibly deriving an erroneous interpretation. If not for the Church's assistance, we'd be as confused as the eunuch struggling to read the Book of Isaiah.

Lord, help us to appreciate your guidance as we read the Bible. Give us the desire to learn the Church's teaching in order to better hear your voice through the pages of sacred Scripture. Amen.

CHAPTER 2

Despair

What am I going to do?

Have you ever asked yourself this question? I certainly have, and I'm sure that I'm not alone. It usually gets uttered when everything in your life looks dark and hopeless. You could be unemployed and looking for work, grieving over the death of a spouse, feeling the pain of a broken relationship or struggling to overcome a personal weakness or addiction. Some people look at the state of the world and begin to fear that even the Church will one day disappear. If we look at these difficulties from a worldly perspective, it's easy to fall victim to despair. When we allow God to speak to us through the pages of sacred Scripture, however, we hear a different message—*never give up!*

While Jesus never promised a life free of problems, he did promise that he will provide the grace we need to endure. We should pray daily for an increase in the virtue of hope. One of the three theological virtues, Christian hope is more than just crossing your fingers and pulling for a positive outcome. According to the *Catechism of the Catholic Church*: "Hope is the theological virtue by which we desire the kingdom of heaven and eternal life as our happiness, placing our trust in Christ's promises and relying not on our own strength, but on the help of the grace of the Holy Spirit" (*CCC* 1817).

In the following Bible verses, the Lord reminds us that there is never a reason to despair. It may not look like it, it may not feel like it, and we may have to focus on the next life, but there is always hope.

8.

"We know that all things work for good for those who love God, who are called according to his purpose" (Romans 8:28).

Obviously, this verse must exclude bad things, correct? After all, how could evil and tragedy be part of God's plan? If we examine this statement closer, however, it definitely says "all things," not some things, not just the good things. Therefore, Saint Paul must really mean it when he states that *all* things work for good for those who love God.

All too often, we complain when things go wrong in our lives. We grumble and cry out for relief from our problems. Why did God do this to me? I'm weak and I can't handle it! What did I do wrong? What we often fail to realize is that these difficulties are actually the rungs on our ladder to heaven. The Lord knows exactly what we need in order to achieve our salvation, and it often involves suffering. Properly handling tribulations is what differentiates a saint from a sinner.

This life is not meant to be a problem-free paradise. The fact that we are Christians doesn't exclude us from suffering. In fact, Jesus said, "If anyone wishes to come after me, he must deny himself and take up his cross daily and follow me" (Luke 9:23). Doesn't sound like followers of Christ are exempt from suffering, does it? While this may be difficult to accept, we can take consolation in Saint Paul's reassurance that everything does work out for the best. With these words, God is saying, "Trust Me, everything will work out in the end." Do we believe these words? Of course we do, at least until something bad happens in our lives.

We should always remember that God can bring good out of evil. Looking at a crucifix reminds us of that fact. When God is in charge, everything really does work out for the best. Even though things may look bleak and hopeless, we can take comfort in the fact that everything that happens to us can help us to achieve our salvation. Everything! There are no exceptions.

My late mother-in-law loved this verse and quoted it often. When problems arose and members of our family would begin to panic, Mom would simply say, "All things work for the good." Simply put, God knows what is good for us, even if it doesn't make sense at the moment. Though these words were not always what any of us wanted to hear, we needed to hear them.

God wants everyone to be saved (1 Timothy 2:4) and stacks the deck in our favor by allowing a unique set of circumstances to occur in each of our lives. Some of these events are pleasant and some are unpleasant, but they are all tailored to fit our own personalities. Properly responding to these happenings will allow us to one day live in eternal paradise. What exactly is the proper response to tragedies and difficulties in our daily lives? Trust, perseverance and prayer are certainly a good start. Do you find it difficult to trust? Yes? Sometimes I do, too. Learning to recognize God's presence in all things, good and bad, can be difficult and is not achieved overnight. By turning to the Lord daily in prayer and asking for an increase in faith, we will find it easier to trust in God's plan. Then, recalling Saint Paul's words to the Romans, we'll comfort ourselves with the knowledge that all things truly work for good!

> *Lord, help us remember that you can always bring good out of evil. Increase our trust in your holy will, even when it involves pain and suffering. Amen.*

9.

"For God so loved the world that he gave his only Son, so that everyone who believes in him might not perish but might have eternal life" (John 3:16).

John 3:16 is easily one of the most popular verses in the Bible. In fact, it's so well-known that we may have become desensitized to its message. We see this verse at sporting events, on websites, and on greeting cards, reminding us of just how much God loves us. What we often fail to recognize, however, is the depth and power of this message. When we begin to fall into despair, this is one of the best verses upon which to meditate. It reminds us that, no matter how bad things look in our lives, there is a light at the end of the tunnel.

Let's begin by thinking about God's love for each of us. Despite the fact that your life may be a complete mess and that everything looks bleak, you can take consolation in the knowledge that God loves you. How great is that love? It's so great that God allowed his only begotten Son to become man and be rejected and crucified so that you can one day go to heaven. Had the Lord not done this, our eternal happiness would not be possible. Now that's what I call love!

No matter how bad your problems are, they will disappear one day. While there is no guarantee that they will be gone in this life, they're not going to follow you after death. Monumental crosses such as unemployment, serious illness, loneliness, and financial difficulties cease once you pass away. Although it might not feel like it, these situations are temporary. What will last forever is the eternal happiness found in the heavenly kingdom.

So what's the catch? What do we have to do to ensure that we end up in heaven? The answer is simple and can be found in this verse. We must believe in Jesus. No problem! All Christians believe in Jesus, so arriving at our heavenly destination should be a done deal, right? In reality, it's not quite that automatic. In order to fully understand the message of this verse, we need to look at what it means to "believe" in Jesus.

Belief in Jesus is more than just acknowledging the biographical details of Christ's life. It also entails that we obey his commands and follow the teachings of the Church. If we say we believe in someone, then it is only logical that we would believe in what he says and does. Jesus founded the Catholic Church (Matthew 16:18) and promised that the Holy Spirit would guide it (John 14:16). If we truly believe in Jesus, we must follow Church teachings and Christ's instructions to "love one another" (John 13:34) and share our riches with those in need (Matthew 19:21). By obeying his words, we truly show that we believe in Jesus. It is that belief that will allow us to one day participate in the heavenly banquet and experience total joy.

Jesus, we thank you for becoming human so that we could live forever with you in heaven. Give us the grace to look beyond our earthly problems and anticipate the eternal happiness that awaits us when we follow your commands. Amen.

10.

"Though your sins be like scarlet, they may become white as snow; though they be red like crimson, they may become white as wool" (Isaiah 1:18).

One of the greatest causes of despair in our lives is when we believe that our sins are unforgivable. Though this position might be the result of a penitent heart, we are mistaken when we do not believe in God's power to heal our souls. No matter what we've done, the Lord is *always* willing to forgive our offenses.

Let's first look at the big picture. When God created Adam and Eve, they lived in paradise and all was well. The Lord gave Adam permission to eat from any of the trees in the Garden except for the tree of knowledge of good and evil (Genesis 2:16–17). Furthermore, the Lord fully explained the consequences of eating from the forbidden tree—death. While it sounds like following God's instructions should have been simple, the allure of the fruit and some slick talk from the evil serpent proved too much for Adam and Eve's willpower. They ate the forbidden fruit and thus lost the right to live in paradise. And their actions affected all future generations.

However, God promised, out of infinite mercy, to send a Savior in reparation for their sinfulness (Genesis 3:15). This Savior, Jesus Christ, was "handed over for our transgressions and was raised for our justification" (Romans 4:25), thus reopening the gates of heaven. Still, we often take the Lord's generosity for granted by contributing our own personal sins (*actual sin*) to those inherited from Adam and Eve (*original sin*). The sacrament of baptism removes all original sin from our souls, but what happens to the "actual" sins we commit?

Fortunately, the Church gives us the sacrament of reconciliation as a means to obtain forgiveness for our sins. Through the prophet Isaiah,

God tells us we can become "white as snow" even though our "sins be like scarlet" (Isaiah 1:18). Want more good news? There is no limit to how many times you can receive this outpouring of God's forgiveness!

While the sacrament of reconciliation is necessary for the forgiveness of mortal sins, it can also be helpful in the battle against lesser (or "venial") sins. If you're like me, you probably have one or two sins that you commit more frequently. Even though these sins may not be grave offenses, you think of them as being impossible to overcome. While not being strictly necessary, "confession of everyday faults (venial sins) is nevertheless strongly recommended by the Church" (CCC 1458), allowing us to smooth out some of our rough edges and become more Christ-like.

God knows that it's often difficult for us to be good and therefore gives us some help. Through the sacrament of reconciliation, we can obtain forgiveness for our offenses and receive the grace to be better people. Don't let this gift go unused!

....

Thank you, Lord, for giving us an infinite number of "second chances" to restore the rift created by our sins. Give us an increased desire to seek forgiveness through the sacrament of reconciliation. Amen.

....

11.

"But as it is written: 'What eye has not seen, and ear has not heard, and what has not entered the human heart, what God has prepared for those who love him'" (1 Corinthians 2:9).

It's not easy to look past the problems that bombard us daily. If you're out of work and have no money in the bank, the monthly mortgage bill can be a cause for panic. If you or a loved one has just been diagnosed with cancer, remaining calm often borders on the impossible. When your spouse or child has just died, finding a "silver lining" may not be very realistic. Using earthly standards, I would agree that any of these situations could be a cause for despair. Thankfully, as Christians, our happiness does not revolve around earthly standards. As Saint Paul reminds us in his first Letter to the Corinthians, the joy that awaits us in the next life is beyond all comprehension.

I often like to meditate on the transfiguration (Matthew 17:1–8, Mark 9:2–8, Luke 9:28–36). In a foretaste of what awaits them in heaven, Jesus allows Peter, James, and John to see him in his heavenly glory. In each of the evangelists' accounts, this incident is sandwiched between the same two events: our Lord's command that his followers must carry a cross and the prediction of his death. Without a doubt, either one of these teachings could have been enough to bring a state of depression upon the apostles. Knowing this, our Lord gave them a foretaste of his glory. It served as a reminder that this life and its difficulties are temporary.

In the same way, we sometimes get so caught up in our suffering that we fail to see what lay ahead of us in Christ. Although we might believe that heaven will be great, it does seem distant and difficult to fathom. Let's see...we won't have material possessions, there will be no football games or TV, and we won't need to eat (though we can, as Jesus did after the resurrection). Instead, we'll experience total happiness by worshiping God all day. And face it, for most of us, the idea of being "in church" 24/7 for all eternity doesn't necessarily cause us to jump for joy. That is understandable and doesn't mean that you don't love God. Rather, it serves as a reminder that we are incapable of fully understanding what life beyond death is like.

When my wife and I got married in 1994, we struggled with infertility. Expecting to have a large family, this was a difficult time for both of us. Eileen was especially affected by this condition, having desired to be a mother for as long as she could remember. During this trying time, she would listen to the song *Eye Has Not Seen* by Marty Haugen (we sang it often at Mass) and would experience peace. Though we could not understand or *see* the way, we knew God was accompanying us. No matter how bad things get "down here," something great awaits us in heaven. How great? We can't even begin to imagine.

Jesus, increase our desire for eternal life in heaven. Help us to want to do whatever it takes to get there and live forever with you. Amen.

12.

"And so I say to you, you are Peter, and upon this rock I will build my church, and the gates of the netherworld shall not prevail against it" (Matthew 16:18).

Most of us feel a lot more peaceful when things are stable. We like to know what to expect, even when the events may be unpleasant. Change can be one of the most anxiety-producing events in our lives, yet many have commented that it is actually the one *constant* on which we can depend. A company I worked for used to "shake things up" every April. Some individuals would be transferred to new locations, others would be assigned to different positions, and a few were even laid off. As the time drew near, we would all speculate on the upcoming changes. Finally, we would see closed office doors and know that the day had arrived. Within a few hours, the changes would be revealed and we would begin the process of adjusting to the modifications. Even though we may have been impacted in some way, we felt a sense of relief and knew that the big changes were finished for the year. A sense of stability had been restored to our lives.

We live in a world that is constantly changing. Businesses come and go, our favorite athletes retire, friends and family pass away... nothing stays the same. In reality, however, that statement is not entirely accurate. Two thousand years ago, Jesus Christ founded the Catholic Church and appointed Saint Peter as its earthly leader. The Church has provided, and will continue to provide, a place of refuge in the midst of an ever-changing world.

In addition to providing a sense of stability in our often unstable lives, the Church serves a more important function. In order to understand this purpose, let's first look at a basic question. Why did Jesus need to establish a Church? Without getting into any advanced theology, Christ did so to help us get to heaven. The Lord knew that we would encounter many obstacles along the way. Therefore, Christ founded a Church to teach us how to lead a holy life and to dispense the graces (through the sacraments) needed to live those teachings.

Our Lord's words to Saint Peter in Matthew 16:18 are clear and should provide a source of comfort to all. Times change, people change, but the Church will continue to bear the good news for all time. In a world filled with temptations and danger, we are blessed by the guidance of the Church, preventing us from losing our way.

Like a lighthouse guiding ships on their way, the Church helps us arrive safely in the heavenly kingdom. May we never fail to avail ourselves of her assistance, especially when surrounded by darkness. Amen.

13.

"Then call on me on the day of distress; I will rescue you, and you shall honor me" (Psalm 50:15).

How often do you ask God to assist you in solving problems? And at what point do you ask for the help? Here is an example of how many of us handle difficult situations in our lives. We encounter a crisis, panic; come up with a solution, panic; ask some people for advice, panic; try something, panic; search the Internet for more options and try some of these ideas, panic BIG TIME and, finally, ask the Lord for help! Why is it that we generally turn to the Lord only after we've exhausted all other options?

Many of us are so accustomed to handling problems on our own that we don't even think about saying a prayer before we begin running around like "chickens with our heads cut off." Whether it's a family illness, a home maintenance issue, or a problem at work, my first instinct is to panic and try lots of different approaches. Fortunately, I have gotten a little better and will now say a prayer before launching into full-blown headless chicken mode. I'm still a "work in progress," however, and I'll be working on this for a long time.

Don't believe me? Last night my wife told me there was a puddle of water in the basement. This is not the first time, as it always occurs during periods of heavy rain. Unfortunately, it hasn't rained at all in the past ten days. After cleaning up the water, I looked for leaking pipes and found no evidence of any. My assumption was that we either had a leak in the main water line or an underground stream had suddenly become active. Although I don't know much about home repairs, I do know that neither of these scenarios would be a good thing. Fortunately, I did remember to pray as I ran up and down the stairs checking for new water and it helped....I felt somewhat peaceful (not a lot of peace, but more than I usually feel). At Eileen's suggestion, I disconnected the garden hose, which was leaking a little bit. After a restless night characterized by more prayer and worry, I woke up and the basement was dry. It was the garden hose! I thanked the Lord and was able to go to the office knowing I wouldn't come home to an unwanted indoor swimming pool.

Besides remembering to ask for the Lord's help, we should never forget to say "thank you." All too often, we forget about God once our crisis subsides. Additionally, we should strive to have an ongoing relationship with the Lord, even when things are going well in our lives. Though God is always there for us in our time of need, the Lord wants to be a part of all aspects of our lives—sorrows and joys. Can you imagine calling your close friends only when you needed something? A true friendship is based on a lot more than constantly asking for favors. If we desire a closer friendship with the Lord, speaking frequently in prayer is a must!

Lord, help us to remember to pray during good times and bad. Although we know that you're always there in our hour of need, we want you to be a part of our lives always...even when things are going well. Amen.

14.

"Jesus said to them, 'I am the bread of life; whoever comes to me will never hunger, and whoever believes in me will never thirst'" (John 6:35).

Due to a variety of circumstances, we can sometimes get discouraged. Thinking that things will never get better, this discouragement can progress to full-blown despair. We can become so overwhelmed with our problems that we just don't see a way out. Although God assures us through Scripture that we will never be abandoned, often we are so blinded by our worries that we fail to listen. In addition to the Lord's presence in sacred Scripture, God is spiritually present to us at all times. We can speak to him while walking, driving, or at the office. Unfortunately, this often gets forgotten in the heat of battle. Sometimes our minds are racing so fast or we're so discouraged that we forget to open our Bible or say a prayer. Knowing human nature as he does, Jesus provides an additional method of assistance that surpasses all other methods. What is this method used by our Lord? His Real Presence in the Eucharist!

Assume for a minute that you have to travel to a remote location, away from friends and family. While there, you are required to make an important decision and need some help. You send an e-mail to a loved one and receive a response. While the reply helps you make your decision and removes some of the feelings of loneliness, can you imagine how much better you'd feel if the response came in the form of a phone call? Hearing the voice of someone you love can be very comforting and is a lot more personal than an e-mail. Imagine your joy if you heard a knock at your door and saw your loved one standing there! Although we can use various methods of electronic communication, nothing comforts us as much as a visit from a close friend.

While Jesus never promised to take away all our difficulties, he did promise to remain with us always (Matthew 28:20). In the Eucharist, Jesus makes good on that promise. Although his outward appearance is different, the same Lord and Savior who walked the earth 2,000 years ago is fully present under the appearance of ordinary bread and wine. Even when words fail us and our thoughts are jumbled and confused, we can receive Christ's Body and Blood in holy Communion. Doing so will bring us grace and peace. When his followers asked for the bread that "gives life to the world" (John 6:33), Jesus far surpassed their request. Instead of simply agreeing to supply the bread, the Lord goes a step further and states that he *is* the bread. That same invitation applies to each of us. Receiving our Lord often will not only provide comfort in times of stress but will help us to make decisions in accordance with God's will.

Thank you, Lord, for your presence in the Eucharist. May we always remember to seek you out in times of trouble, confident that we will receive the graces necessary to continue our battle.

CHAPTER 3

Doubt

Having been a computer programmer for most of my life, I know the joy that comes with watching your code work properly. For many programmers, the happiness is usually accompanied by a feeling of surprise: *Hey, my program actually works!* Those of you who have unpacked a new computer or electronic device may have experienced a similar feeling when you plugged it in and it functioned right out of the box. Whether we call it being skeptical, cynical, or realistic, we don't expect many things in life to go smoothly. Unfortunately, we often view our relationship with God this way. Despite what the Bible teaches us about answered prayer and God's power, we frequently doubt the Lord's ability to "come through" when we need something.

We know that nothing is impossible with God (Luke 1:37) and that Jesus performed many miracles, but will the Lord really help me find a job or heal my cancer-stricken mother? As further evidence, how do we react when God does respond positively to one of our requests? Usually, we're shocked and amazed. Why? Probably because we didn't expect our prayer to be answered! If we had confidence in God, why would we be surprised when our request was granted?

Having confidence in God doesn't mean that we always expect a "yes" from the Lord. There are times when we ask for things that could hurt us spiritually. In his infinite wisdom, the Lord may protect us by answering "no" to our prayer. Rather than always expecting to receive what we request, we should focus on learning to believe that God can do all things. This attitude will allow us to pray with greater confidence. The verses in this chapter will help us recall that "for God all things are possible" (Matthew 19:26).

15.

"And I tell you, ask and you will receive; seek and you will find; knock and the door will be opened to you" (Luke 11:9).

This is one of those Bible verses that can either bring us comfort or drive us crazy! In my younger days, I viewed Jesus' statement as the equivalent of the genie in the bottle's "your wish is my command." When my prayer request wasn't granted, however, it was a totally different story. I did what the Lord said, but God did not deliver. Could I have misunderstood Christ's words? In reality, that's exactly what happened. When understood properly, these words can greatly increase our confidence in God's ability to provide for our needs.

When I was in college, a wise priest explained this verse to me by saying that God will always say "yes" if we ask for the right things. His recommendation was to pray for the wisdom to ask for those things which God wants me to have. In my twenty-year-old mind, I thought it was the ultimate cop-out. If the Lord is only going to give me what he wants, then what's the point of asking for anything? As incomprehensible as it was to me at the time, however, Father Dave's answer was right on the money. If we ask the Lord for "good things," he is going to grant our request. This means we are praying in accordance with the Lord's will.

Because we are human and subject to many imperfections, it's not always easy to discern God's will. Because of this, we must be prepared to accept God's answer even if it's not what we want. While most of us are aware of Jesus' "ask and you shall receive" comment, we sometimes overlook the words that follow:

"What father among you would hand his son a snake when he asks for a fish? Or hand him a scorpion when he asks for an egg? If you then, who are wicked, know how to give good gifts to your children, how much more will the Father in heaven give the holy Spirit to those who ask him?" (Luke 11:11-13).

While we will definitely "receive" when we ask, the Lord does not promise that we will receive *what* we want, *when* we want it. If granted, some of our requests could prove to be damaging to our spiritual life. The new job with a greater salary could cause us to become more materialistic and abandon God in favor of additional possessions. The sought-after relationship with a certain person may lead us to a sinful lifestyle. Ultimately it's very possible that these "answered prayers" could even jeopardize our salvation. Although we may not realize it at the time, God has our best interests at heart and will answer our prayers accordingly.

If understood correctly, Jesus' promise of "ask and you shall receive" is a reassuring guarantee of divine providence. With these words, we can rest assured that the Lord will hear and answer our prayers. Our job is to ask. His job is to decide how to answer and when.

Dear Jesus, help remove the doubt from our minds as we turn to you with our intentions. Increase our trust in your divine providence and allow our will to be aligned with yours. Amen.

16.

"Trust in the LORD forever! For the LORD is an eternal Rock" (Isaiah 26:4).

The words "In God We Trust" are very familiar and even appear on United States currency. If you surveyed a number of Christians and asked if they trust God, most of them would probably answer "yes." Based on this response, how do you think one of these individuals would react to the tragic death of a family member or a serious illness? Chances are good that they wouldn't be peaceful. There is also the distinct possibility that the reaction might even involve anger toward God. While these emotions are understandable considering the situation, they indicate a problem—lack of trust in God.

Genuine trust in God involves acceptance of all events, pleasant and unpleasant, that occur in our lives. We've all encountered those holy people who remain unshaken when things go wrong in their lives, believing that God is with them in times of sorrow and distress. While this attitude is not the norm, even among Christians, striving to trust in the Lord is critical in the Christian journey.

Before I go any further, let me go on the record and say that I fall into this "lack of trust" category more often than I'd like to admit. Every time I find myself worrying about my family or allowing episodes of anxiety to rule my life, I'm reminded that my faith isn't what it should be. Incidentally, when I say "worrying about my family," I'm not referring to taking care of their needs. Instead I'm speaking of useless speculation about potential problems that *could* affect them one day. When I find myself slipping into "worry mode," I know it's time to hit my knees and pray for an increase in faith.

The Apostle Thomas is sometimes referred to as the patron saint of doubters. Better known as "Doubting Thomas," he is generally remembered for his skepticism about Christ's resurrection (John

20:25). After Thomas expressed doubt, Jesus made another visit to the apostles and allowed him to examine his wounds (John 20:27). Upon doing so, the now-believing apostle cried out, "My Lord and My God!" Let's examine the Lord's actions. When Thomas had doubts, Jesus appeared and helped him to believe. Like Thomas, you and I often have doubts about the Lord's plans for our lives. Things happen that just don't make sense and we often lose confidence in God's providence. When this happens, we would be wise to take a page out of Thomas' book and cry out to the Lord for help. Just as he appeared to Thomas, Jesus will draw near to each of us and grant us peace. We can find him in the pages of the Bible, the sacraments, the teachings of the Church, and even in the advice of a wise friend. Despite the fact that we don't fully understand why things are happening, the Lord can help us to better accept them.

....

Lord, help us remember the importance of asking for your help in times of doubt and confusion. Like the Apostle Thomas, may we always recognize your presence in our lives and loudly exclaim, "My Lord and My God!" Amen.

....

17.

"Therefore I tell you, all that you ask for in prayer, believe that you will receive it and it shall be yours" (Mark 11:24).

One of the most difficult tasks we face as Christians is to believe that the Lord can perform miracles. I'm not talking about miracles in the Bible, but miracles in our own lives. If your husband is diagnosed with terminal cancer, do you believe that Jesus can heal him? If you've been out of work for several months and have been rejected for dozens of positions, do you believe that the Lord can allow you to find a job? Generally speaking, this kind of belief is not easy. Why? Because the world tells us that believing in miracles is not realistic.

Several months ago, I received an e-mail requesting prayers for a pregnant woman named Melissa who had just been diagnosed with an aggressive form of breast cancer. In an effort to save the lives of Melissa and her child, the doctors suggested delivering the baby early in order to begin treating the cancer with chemotherapy and radiation. As would be expected, this mother-to-be was devastated by the news. I immediately posted the prayer request on a social network, and many people started to pray for a positive outcome. A few days later I received news that the doctors revised the plan and were able to completely remove the tumor. In addition, it was discovered that the cancer hadn't spread as originally believed. Melissa was cancer-free! Was this a miracle? It sure looks that way to me. Did I think that God could heal her? I most certainly did. How could I be so sure?

In August 1997, while expecting our first child (or so we thought), my wife and I were given some good news and some terrible news. First, we were informed that we were having twins. A few hours after that, we were stunned to hear that there was a serious problem with our children. In the days that followed, the news grew worse. The girls were not expected to live. The first thing that we did was to give them names. We chose the names Mary and Elizabeth in honor of the Blessed Mother and her cousin. The second thing we did was pray A LOT! We were desperate and needed a miracle. In order to spread the word, we wrote letters to the local newspaper and called radio shows. A great many people prayed for the girls and their dangerous situation. As a result, Eileen and I felt a supernatural peace descend upon us. Although we didn't know how things would turn out, we knew that God was in charge. I remember thinking that, although I don't know if the girls *will* be healed, I need to believe that God *can* heal them.

After much prayer, I did indeed believe. Ever since that day, I've never doubted the Lord's ability to perform miracles.

In our case, Mary and Elizabeth were physically healed of their condition. I have prayed for other people, however, who did not recover from their illnesses. While it's important for us to believe in the Lord's healing power, we must also trust hiss judgment. God knows when a physical healing is the best option for those involved. Sometimes the Lord decides that what is needed is a spiritual healing. Through prayer and reception of the sacraments, we will come to believe that God will always answer our prayers in the best way possible.

Lord, help us to always pray with confidence, knowing that you can do all things. Increase our faith so we can trust your judgment, knowing your will is perfect. Amen.

18.

"The Lord replied, 'If you have faith the size of a mustard seed, you would say to [this] mulberry tree, 'Be uprooted and planted in the sea,' and it would obey you'" (Luke 17:6).

When asked by the apostles to increase their faith, Jesus replied with this familiar statement regarding faith and a mustard seed. As you may be aware, mustard seeds are very small but grow into large plants. If we read between the lines, the Lord appears to be telling the apostles that they are not making use of the faith that they already have. This message applies to each one of us. While praying for an increase in faith is certainly a recommend practice, are we making use of what we've already been given?

When I was a child, I loved to eat at buffet restaurants. Unfortunately, I would also take more food than I could eat. Trying to discourage me from being wasteful, my parents would correct me and comment that, "my eyes were bigger than my stomach." They wanted me to learn that I should finish what was on my plate before getting new items. While most adults understand this concept when it comes to food, there is still a lot of confusion when it comes to faith.

All Christians have been gifted with some degree of faith. It allows us to believe in God and things that are unseen (Hebrews 11:1). However, faith isn't meant to be a strictly intellectual activity. Faith is meant to be lived. In the Bible, Saint James clearly tells us that "faith of itself, if it does not have works, is dead" (James 2:17). Having faith in God is a gift and should spur us on to perform good works such as prayer and almsgiving.

Although it's true that we must strive to put our faith into action, the good news is that even the smallest amount of faith is enough to move mountains. By all means we should continue to ask the Lord to increase our faith, but we must never forget to make use of the faith we already have by praying frequently and with confidence. By doing so, an outpouring of graces and blessings will be unleashed...even if our faith is as small as a mustard seed.

....

Dear Lord, help us to remember the importance of prayer in our lives. Grant us the grace to pray with confidence, knowing that even the smallest amount of faith can result in miracles. Amen.

....

19.

"And we have this confidence in him, that if we ask anything according to his will, he hears us" (1 John 5:14).

Have you ever wondered if God is really listening to your prayers? It is a common question and usually gets raised when our prayers aren't answered satisfactorily. Looking at the above Bible verse can confuse us even more. Is Saint John actually saying there are occasions when God doesn't hear our prayers? Fortunately for us, that is not the case. Although the translation of this verse can be confusing, the Lord always hears our prayers but grants our desires according to his will. Given that fact, the importance of discerning God's will becomes clear. How do we know that we are asking "according to his will," and what can we do if we're not sure?

Determining God's will for your life is a worthwhile pursuit. Why? If you desire to follow God's will, it makes it easier if you know what the Lord wants you to do. For instance, if you knew for sure that God wanted you to be a wife and mother, it wouldn't make sense to pray for acceptance into a convent. Unfortunately, although we may have a good idea of God's will for our lives, we can never be certain. This uncertainty can be overcome by appending a few words to all of your prayers. Every time you pray for something, I recommend that you close the prayer by adding the words, "if it's your will." By doing this, you'll be submitting to the Lord's will and imitating Jesus' prayer on the night before his death: "He advanced a little and fell prostrate in prayer, saying, 'My Father, if it is possible, let this cup pass from me; yet, not as I will, but as you will'" (Matthew 26:39).

Although praying in this way eliminates a lot of the guesswork, we should still refrain from requests that are obviously not in accord with God's will. This would include anything that violates a teaching of the Church. For instance, it wouldn't be a good practice to pray for the success of an adulterous affair or ask for God's blessing on an illegal gambling endeavor. Praying for these intentions would be an insult to the Lord and should be avoided.

While we may never understand *how* prayer works, we do know that it *does* work. More importantly, it is a necessary component of our spiritual life. Jesus prayed frequently and often emphasized the need for prayer. The more we pray, the better we get to know the Lord. As our relationship with the Lord grows, so does our confidence that God always hears and answers our prayers.

Teach us, O Lord, to desire your will for our lives. When we are tempted to feel that you aren't listening, help us remember that you always desire what's best for us, and sometimes that means saying, "no." Amen.

20.

"Whatever you ask for in prayer with faith, you will receive" (Matthew 21:22).

While returning to the city one day, Jesus encountered a fig tree by the road. He was hungry and looked for fruit on the tree. Finding nothing but leaves, the Lord cursed the tree and stated that it will never again bear fruit. Immediately, the tree withered and the disciples were amazed. Sensing their astonishment at what happened to the fig tree, Jesus replied: "Amen, I say to you, if you have faith and do not waver, not only will you do what has been done to the fig tree, but even if you say to this mountain, 'Be lifted up and thrown into the sea,' it will be done" (Matthew 21:21).

In order to drive home the point, the Lord concluded his comments with the message above: "Whatever is prayed for with faith will be received." At first glance, this incident can be a bit confusing. What is the point of this story, and why did I include it in a chapter on doubt? As with most of Jesus' lessons, there are a few messages here, and understanding them requires some effort on our part.

In a sense, we are all fig trees and are expected to bear fruit in our lives. Unlike edible fruit that can be consumed, our "fruit" is represented by good works. Instead of being totally self-centered, we are expected to do nice things for others. The Church teaches that when we die, we will be judged. If we led a good life and remained faithful to Christ, we will spend eternity with God in heaven. Bearing good fruit in our lives will ultimately result in eternal happiness. Jesus teaches us that like the fig tree, if we fail to be fruitful, we will be cut off from life in God.

Although the lesson about bearing fruit is an important one, the disciples couldn't get past the fact that the Jesus' words caused the fig tree to dry up. Addressing their amazement, the Lord chose to make a statement about the power of faith. Taking the focus away from himself, he basically told them, "You can do this, too, if you have faith." When we hear this talk of moving mountains and cursing fig trees, we tend to brush it off for two reasons. We either feel that our faith is too weak (and leave it at that) or assume that Jesus is speaking figuratively and proceed to ignore the message. Both of these approaches are problematic and will cause us to miss the main "take-away" of the lesson.

Rather than get distracted by the details, we should focus on the power of faith. When we pray with faith, great things can happen. Meditating upon this will give us a greater desire and appreciation for the gift of faith. We should be willing to do whatever we can so that our faith can grow. How can we increase our faith? We should pray frequently for an increase of this gift. As a result, we'll be able to move mountains in our own lives.

Lord, we desire to "move mountains" and know that it can only be accomplished by praying with faith. Please increase this gift in our lives so that, with your help, we can do great things. Amen.

21.

"And he said, 'What is impossible for human beings is possible for God'" (Luke 18:27).

There's no doubt about it, life is difficult. Every day we are faced with numerous obstacles that can cause us to become beaten down. Even more difficult is living a good *Christian* life. Why? Because in addition to the ordinary problems that complicate our lives, we must also fight off the temptations that bombard us throughout the day. As followers of the Lord, we are expected to rise above these distractions and faithfully walk the road that leads to eternal life in heaven.

How are we expected to behave? In the Sermon on the Mount, Jesus told us to be perfect, as our heavenly Father is perfect (Matthew 5:48). Calling this a difficult task would rank as a colossal understatement. Some will view it as being impossible and argue that there's no way we can live a life of perfection in an imperfect world. I would agree, *if* we try to do this by ourselves. Fortunately for us, God doesn't expect us to do this alone. The Lord knows that we are weak and that it's impossible for us to be good all the time. Therefore, God is prepared to give us the grace needed to live a holy life and overcome the obstacles that stand in our way. With this grace, the impossible suddenly becomes possible.

The Bible constantly reminds us that nothing is impossible for God. Given that fact, why do we view certain situations as hopeless? Generally speaking, it's because we don't think the Lord is going to do the impossible in our lives. If Scripture tells us the Lord can do all things, why is this so difficult for us to accept? More importantly, how can it be fixed? For starters, one option is to spend more time reading the Bible. Frequent reading of Scripture is a necessary spiritual practice for all Christians. One of my hopes for this book is that it will get people used to "hearing" God speak through the pages of the Bible. Whether or not we have a major crisis in our life, we should get into the habit of encountering the Lord in this way. This will help us to believe that God can do the impossible and inspire us to pray with confidence at all times.

Dear Lord, thank you for speaking to us through the pages of the Bible. Help us to develop a greater understanding and love for your written word. Along with this, please increase our confidence in your ability to "do the impossible." Amen.

CHAPTER 4

Fear

Several years ago, before I was married, I visited Disney World with my best friend Chuck. While neither of us were thrill seekers, we decided to ride on Space Mountain. I'm not sure how or why we committed to doing this, but I think it had something to do with neither of us wanting to admit that we were afraid of a ride. As we stood in line, we joked about how it wouldn't be as frightening as a regular roller coaster because of the fact that we'd be in the dark (famous last words). As we arrived at the front of the line, I started to get nervous and made the comment, "I hope you know that I'm just doing this because you wanted to." Chuck responded by saying, "Me? I thought you wanted to do it!" As we stood there looking at each other, the silence was broken by the ticket taker's words: "Next!"

Though thrill seeking might be an exception (horror movies, haunted houses and roller coasters), generally being afraid is not fun. In fact, out of all the potential causes of anxiety in life, many will say that fear is the worst. In cases such as illness, unemployment, uncertainty, and commitment, fear results from lack of control. We are most comfortable when we believe that we are in control of our lives. When that feeling is disrupted, we tend to be afraid.

In the installation homily of his pontificate, Blessed Pope John Paul II cautioned against fear three times. In quoting the famous words of

Jesus ("Be not afraid"), the late Holy Father called to mind the many times the Lord proclaimed the uselessness of fear. Unfortunately, fear still remains a part of many lives. As we continue to fight this battle in our daily lives, may we learn to seek comfort in the word of God.

22.

"I should like you to be free of anxieties" (1 Corinthians 7:32).

My father passed away in 2002, and I think of him often. Although I try to remember his words and hear the sound of his voice, it gets more difficult as the years go by. Memories become blurred and even forgotten with each new day. I usually visit Dad's grave a few times during the year in order to pray for his soul and talk with him. After all, one of the great teachings of our Catholic faith is that life doesn't end with death. Although this may sound trivial, one of the benefits that I get from visiting my father's grave is being able to read his name on the tombstone. When I see the inscription "Edward Zimak, 1922–2002," something special happens. Being able to visually see his name brings a flood of memories, and I can feel Dad's presence. All because of some written words.

Saint Paul's message to the people of Corinth couldn't be clearer. In fact, the statement that he wants them to be free of anxieties seems so obvious that we want to brush it off as being nothing more than fluff. Doing so, however, would be a big mistake. The Church teaches that God is the ultimate author of the Bible. Therefore, although Saint Paul penned this message to the Corinthians, God inspired him to do so. The Lord is telling us that it is his desire for us to be free from anxieties. Although this is probably not a big revelation to anyone, reading and rereading these words can be an effective technique for eliminating our fear. Just as seeing my father's name is a comfort to me, reading this message from the Lord can give us a great deal of peace.

You may question the necessity of repeatedly hearing an obvious message. Is there really anyone who believes that God *does* want them to be anxious? Let's look at an example. I know that my wife loves me, and she knows that I love her. Therefore, what's the point of us saying "I love you" to each other several times each day? Anyone who's ever heard those words knows the point. We never grow tired of hearing that expression of affection, do we? Our words can make a big difference in someone's life. Knowing that God wants us to be free from anxieties is one thing, but *hearing* the Lord say it several times each day is another. Through the words of Saint Paul in his letter to the Corinthians, we can hear that message from the Lord as many times as we wish.

When you wake up tomorrow and begin to worry, open your Bible to 1 Corinthians 7:32 for a special message from the Lord. If you're struggling an hour later, look at it again. The message remains the same. God doesn't want us to be anxious. Ask for assistance, and the Lord won't let you down.

Thank you for your comforting message, Lord. Help us to cling to your words as we struggle with fear in our daily lives. Amen.

23.

"At once [Jesus] spoke to them, 'Take courage, it is I; do not be afraid'" (Matthew 14:27).

During the summer of 2011, my wife and I decided that we would homeschool our girls for the first time. Before making this decision, we prayed and consulted many people. We felt peaceful for a few months, but that peace began to fade as September approached. Finally, the big day arrived and we were "off to the races." Seventh grade had begun for Mary and Elizabeth. Our feeling at the end of the first day? Complete and total panic! I frantically started thinking of other options and considered everything from finding a good Catholic school to quitting my job and becoming a co-teacher.

It's easy to feel peace when all is going well. Unfortunately, there is no way we're going to get through our lives without experiencing some problems. When these situations occur, we can take comfort in the above words of our Lord. Originally spoken to the apostles as they were in a boat being battered by strong waves and wind, this message is also directed to those of us who struggle with difficulties in our lives.

Saint Peter responded to the Lord's command (Matthew 14:28) and began to walk on the water. All was going well until he made the mistake of concentrating more on the storm than on Jesus. He began to sink. The Lord caught him and asked why he doubted. How many times do we make the same mistake? When faced with unexpected problems, we often panic and find ourselves overcome with fear. We may even try to pray, but abandon that approach as the storms grow more intense. Although it seems counterintuitive, we should try to keep our focus on the Lord and not on the waves crashing around us. Peter was doing fine until he took his eyes off Jesus. We make the same mistake whenever we turn away from the Lord and dwell on the storms in our lives.

Although our first reaction was one of panic, Eileen and I felt better once we started concentrating on the Lord. We reminded ourselves that we prayed about the decision for several months and spoke with many people. In *every* case, the response was positive. We knew that there was no way that God would fool us into making a decision against his will. We are doing much better now, but we still have to fight off the urge to panic. When we begin to feel uneasy, we know that it's time to pray harder.

When we receive Jesus in holy Communion, we have a personal encounter with the same Savior who reassured the Apostles in the midst of the waves. With Jesus, no problem is too great to handle. He is all we need. Meet him frequently in prayer, Scripture, and the Eucharist.

....

Lord, help us to recall your presence when we're being battered by the storms of life. Replace our doubt with peace as we allow you to reign as our Lord and Savior. Amen.

....

24.

"Peace I leave with you; my peace I give to you. Not as the world gives do I give it to you. Do not let your hearts be troubled or afraid" (John 14:27).

If a friend of yours is dealing with a crisis and you caution him or her against being afraid, the odds are good that you'll be met with resistance. You may hear something to the effect of, "Are you kidding me? How can I not be afraid?" Unfortunately, the world tells us that the proper response to uncertainty is fear. Fortunately, this is only the case if we don't allow God into our lives.

As I state throughout this book, I am "hard-wired" to be a worrier. It is my nature to turn molehills into mountains, especially when it comes to health issues. Doctor's visits, blood tests, and unusual symptoms have never been fun experiences for me. Now that I have a wife and kids, the tendency to worry gets multiplied. Every time someone gets a strange headache or needs to get a medical test, my initial reaction is a feeling of uneasiness. Why am I telling you this? I want you to understand that, although I am truly a worrier at heart,

I've discovered the secret to controlling worry in my life. The Lord can remove our anxiety and replace it with peace when we allow it.

What does Jesus mean when he states that his peace is different than that of the world? In order to answer that question, let's look at someone who doesn't believe in God. Imagine that this person has just been diagnosed with a tumor of some kind. There is a very good chance that this news will cause him or her to be afraid, lacking peacefulness. How will this person's sense of peace be restored? Likely, it will only happen if either the tumor is found to be benign or if it is successfully removed; in other words, only if the problem goes away. The Lord's peace, on the other hand, operates in a different way. God's peace is not dependent on external circumstances. There are many cancer patients who turn to the Lord and feel peace even though their physical condition is unchanged.

Unless we come up with a way to find peace in the midst of our troubles, we are going to be miserable for much of our lives. The supernatural peace Jesus promises is what we need. As soon as you encounter a problem in your life, I recommend that you get in the habit of saying a prayer. It doesn't have to be elaborate. A simple "Lord, help me" will suffice. I've learned to do this, and I can assure you that it works. Give it a try and see what happens.

When troubles occur in our lives, Lord, help us ignore the urge to panic. Instead, grant us the grace to turn to you and ask for the supernatural peace that only you can provide. Amen.

25.

"The LORD is my light and my salvation; whom should I fear? The LORD is my life's refuge; of whom should I be afraid?" (Psalm 27:1).

In our daily lives, we are afraid of many things—terrorist attacks, unemployment, illness, and assorted other situations. If the Lord is truly our light and salvation, however, should we really have any fears? Does losing our job or having financial problems affect our salvation? How about being diagnosed with an illness? Losing one or more of our friends? Suffering from a severe bout of loneliness? No! So, why are we afraid of these things?

Like it or not, attachment to earthly possessions and comfort goes along with being human. It's easy to lose sight of the fact that this life isn't the "end of the story." As difficult as it is for us to understand, our true home is heaven, and this life is only temporary. Being human, however, often prevents us from remembering this fact. This Bible passage provides us with a reminder and an important question. It is a question that we should ask ourselves whenever we feel anxious about the things of this world. It should be etched into our memory and repeated when we are being battered by the storms of life. As long as we have a good relationship with God, why should we fear any earthly problem?

Adhering to this way of thinking is only possible by diverting our attention from the world and focusing more on the Lord. In fact, this is one of those verses that should be read and recited frequently. It can become one of our daily prayers and will help us keep things in perspective. Training our minds to focus on eternal life can be an effective method of minimizing fear in this life. Instead of concentrating on the loss of wealth or the inconvenience associated with poor health, we should instead focus on the joy that will await us in heaven.

As we find ourselves surrounded by problems and the forces of evil, we should never fail to seek refuge in the Lord. God will protect us and provide the graces we need. There is no problem or temptation that is greater than God. If we remain close, we will one day reside with the Blessed Trinity in heaven. Meditating on this this idea should bring us great comfort and give us the confidence to withstand any difficulty. With the Lord on our side, there really is *nothing* to fear!

Thank you, Jesus, for becoming man and making our salvation possible. Help us remember that, as long as we remain in the state of grace, we have nothing to fear. Amen.

26.

"Have no anxiety at all, but in everything, by prayer and petition, with thanksgiving, make your requests known to God. Then the peace of God that surpasses all understanding will guard your hearts and minds in Christ Jesus" (Philippians 4:6–7).

"Why worry when you can pray?"

My late mother-in-law was known for saying this whenever we told her that we were worried about something. It was a question that called attention to the useless nature of worry. When we look at Saint Paul's advice to the Philippians, it's hard to justify wasting time worrying. Still, it happens, and part of eliminating this behavior is learning to control our reaction to adversity.

My friend, Tony, likes this verse so much that he reads it every day. When my wife, Eileen, was going through a difficult time in her life, she would also read it frequently. By reading this verse frequently, Eileen and Tony show great wisdom, and we can all learn something from their approach. When we open the Bible, the Lord speaks directly to us. If God tells us to pray and not worry, that's what we should do. If we wake up the next day and feel the urge to worry, then it's time to open our Bible again. If, like Tony, you feel the need to read this every day, then so be it.

Although the main message of this Bible verse is clear, there is a key element that is easy to overlook. How does Saint Paul tell us we should pray? With thanksgiving! That can be simple when we receive a great favor, but it's not so easy when we're going through difficult times. Nonetheless, it is necessary. In his letter to the Thessalonians, Saint Paul says we should "give thanks in all circumstances" (1 Thessalonians 5:18), not just when things are going well. While this can be difficult, doing so allows us to humbly submit to God's will.

If we follow Saint Paul's advice and pray with thanksgiving at all times, what is the reward? The immediate reward is a peace "that surpasses all understanding." More importantly, this kind of attitude will lead you closer to Jesus. As we struggle with the temptation to be anxious, let us instead focus on the God-inspired words of Saint Paul. How often should they be read? As often as necessary.

Jesus, we give you thanks for all of the events in our lives, good as well as bad. Please grant us your peace as we struggle to meet the daily challenges that arise every day. Amen.

27.

"Can any of you by worrying add a single moment to your life-span?"
(Matthew 6:27).

How would you respond if Jesus asked you this question? Rather than dismiss it as a hypothetical question, all of us "worriers" should feel obligated to provide an answer. While the automatic response is "no," the Lord's obvious follow-up question would probably be, "Then why do you worry?"

Some may make the argument that, when faced with a problem, we would be foolish not to analyze our options. This is not the worry Jesus is referring to in the Sermon on the Mount. The kind of action condemned by the Lord is *useless* worry that does nothing but increase our fear. As an example, imagine that your husband or wife has just been diagnosed with a serious illness. While it would be productive to think about the different treatment options (in order to choose the best one), it would be senseless to spend time worrying about how much you'll miss your spouse once the illness (presumably) becomes fatal. The adage of "one day at a time" really comes into play in a situation like this and reminds us to deal with problems *when* they arise, rather than assuming that they *will* arise.

Time spent worrying could be better utilized by prayer and good works. If we find our minds so distracted that prayer becomes difficult, we can turn to formal prayers (such as the Our Father or the Hail Mary) or offer up our work as a prayer. The Lord knows that we are weak and is always ready to help us. Turning to Christ in prayer and asking for assistance can be very effective in eliminating anxiety. We know what he teaches about useless worry, so we can be sure that asking Jesus for help will yield positive results.

When you encounter problems in your life, by all means go ahead and plan a strategy. Just be careful, however, that you're not wasting valuable time fretting over possible outcomes. Always remember that every minute you spend worrying is one less minute you'll spend praying. Considering the Lord's opinion about the uselessness of worry, it is not a good tradeoff!

Lord, help us to remember that worrying is a useless and unproductive waste of our time. In times of trouble, inspire us to turn to you with hope and confidence. Amen.

28.

"Then the angel said to her, 'Do not be afraid, Mary, for you have found favor with God'" (Luke 1:30).

If there was ever a case for fear, this was it! The angel Gabriel appeared to Mary and asked her to become the mother of the long-awaited Savior. The details? It will happen by the power of the Holy Spirit. How would we respond to this invitation? I can honestly see myself saying "No thanks...I'm not the right person for the job," or, "Let me get back to you in a few days." Mary's response? "I am the handmaid of the Lord. May it be done to me according to your word" (Luke 1:38). She had such trust in the will of God that she went along with the plan without knowing most of the details.

For many of us, the "unknown" can be a great source of anxiety. When my father was diagnosed with cancer, he was very nervous about the effects of the chemotherapy and radiation treatments. Would he feel sick? Would he become very weak? Would there be a lot of pain? His anxiety increased as he neared the date of the first chemotherapy session. When the day arrived, I sat with him as the drugs were administered and we spoke about many things. I discussed problems with my job and he offered his wise, fatherly advice. As the minutes passed and he wasn't feeling any worse, he began to relax. Afterward, the entire family celebrated with a big lunch and a nice dessert. Once Dad knew what to expect, he was able to relax (to some extent) because the previously cloudy side effects of the treatment were now known.

While learning the facts can turn fear into peace, we are often asked to face frightening situations *without* knowing the facts. Illness, job loss, marriage difficulties, pregnancy, and many other occurrences are sometimes thrust upon us unexpectedly. Just like Mary, we must sometimes face an uncertain future with few or no details. The secret to experiencing peace in these situations involves trusting in God.

When faced with the unknown, we can take comfort that many, like Mary, have lived with great faith. Mary experienced uncertainty when the angel appeared, but she trusted in the Lord's provisions. Do you find it difficult to say "yes" when facing an unknown future? Mary understands. Ask for her help. You'll be amazed at how much peace you can feel once you stop trying to face your problems all by yourself.

Holy Mary, you trusted in God's plan even when it didn't make sense. Pray for us, that we may develop a greater trust in the Lord's perfect will for our lives. Amen.

CHAPTER 5

Persecution

When we hear the word "persecution," we normally think of an act involving violence. At the very least, the threat of physical harm is implied. If we don't follow a certain set of instructions or live by certain guidelines, someone will harm us in some way. It is a restriction of our right to believe or live as we wish. Persecution comes in many forms and can involve many different threats. One of the most common forms of this practice is religious persecution. When this occurs, individuals are harmed, threatened, or harassed for their religious beliefs. In the United States, we don't see a lot of physical religious persecution, but assuming that persecution doesn't exist would be a mistake. There is much pressure on Catholics (and on all Christians) to abandon their religious beliefs and live the attitude of popular culture, pursuing pleasure and disdaining any rules that stand in the way.

Whether or not we are threatened with physical violence, it is not easy to live our Catholic faith in today's world. The challenges range from subtle persuasion to actual threats. A quick glance at the comments on any online article about the Catholic Church or the editorial page of any major newspaper will quickly confirm this assertion.

With all of this pressure and the threat of violence, how can we be possibly live according to Christ's standards? Fortunately for us, the Lord provides numerous words of wisdom in the pages of the Bible.

The pressures we face have existed for thousands of years, yet the word of God remains the same. No matter how much pressure we face to abandon our religious beliefs, God will provide us with the strength we need to stay the course.

29.

"My foes treat me harshly all the day; yes, many are my attackers. O Most High, when I am afraid, in you I place my trust" (Psalm 56:3–4).

The Liturgy of the Hours, the official daily prayer of the Church, is primarily made up of the psalms. One of the common themes found in the Book of Psalms is the threat of enemy attack. Surviving while being surrounded by foes is a constant theme throughout the Psalter. Initially, I found this theme to be very confusing. Why must we pray for relief from enemies? After all, I didn't think I had any real foes in my life. I couldn't understand why this official prayer of the Church would focus on a concept that didn't pertain to most of the world's Catholics.

Over time, I realized that my daily life really was a battle and that I was surrounded by constant dangers. Despite a lack of visible opponents, we all face a barrage of unseen threats and temptations every day of our lives. The dangerous allure of sin, combined with a love of comfort can provide a lethal blow to our weak human nature. Make no mistake about it: Anyone who tries to follow the Lord's commandments is "at war" every day.

In addition to the unseen threats, our spiritual lives can also be complicated due to the challenges of visible opponents. When you try to live your Catholic faith, you will make many enemies. Even if you are not threatened with physical violence, you can be expected to encounter verbal abuse and criticism. People may question why you believe that abortion is evil, accusing you of opposing "women's rights" or "freedom of choice." Your openness to procreation may be mocked and branded as a form of "Catholic guilt." Belief in dogmatic teachings such as Mary's immaculate conception, purgatory, and Jesus' Real Presence will place you in serious danger of belittlement.

Fortunately for us, the Lord is aware of the dangers we face each day and provides us with the strength we need. Sometimes the gifts of the Holy Spirit are taken for granted, but they can often provide a powerful weapon in our spiritual arsenal. Detailed in the Book of Isaiah (Chapter 11:2–3), these gifts are given to us in order that we may lead a more Christ-like life. When it comes to standing our ground and doing battle with the visible and invisible forces of evil, the gift of fortitude can be a tremendous help. Fortitude, or courage, strengthens us with the ability to do the right thing even when we are threatened physically or verbally. It can provide a degree of immunity against the criticism and insults directed toward us. This gift, combined with all of the other graces that the Lord provides, will allow us to achieve victory over all of our attackers.

Holy Spirit, we ask you to come alive in our souls and protect us from our foes. With your help, may we continue to remain strong in our faith and never lose hope in your protection. Amen.

30.

"You will be hated by all because of my name, but not a hair on your head will be destroyed. By your perseverance you will secure your lives" (Luke 21:17–19).

I can just about guarantee that as soon as you start mentioning Jesus, someone will get annoyed. Need some proof? Take a look at NFL quarterback Tim Tebow, who makes no secret of his love for Jesus. He has been criticized for mentioning the Lord's name but remains true to his beliefs. While people will tolerate our religious beliefs to a point, speaking about Christ will eventually cause a negative response from someone.

You've likely heard the recommendation that religion is one of two things (politics being the other) that shouldn't be discussed in the workplace. Why? Because proclaiming the "Good News" of Jesus Christ causes division. Many individuals aren't open to the Church's moral guidelines, choosing to decide for themselves what they will believe. Even the simple act of verbalizing our own religious beliefs (with no hint of preaching) will cause a backlash, especially if it occurs in the workplace.

Although this negative reaction might not feel good, we can't say we weren't warned. On several occasions, Jesus mentioned that his followers would be hated. No surprise there. We all have our enemies, and we know that some folks don't like religion. What sometimes catches us off-guard, however, is when the hatred comes from an unlikely source. In one of the most challenging passages in all of Scripture, the Lord warns that his teaching will cause division *even within families!*

"Do not think that I have come to bring peace upon the earth. I have come to bring not peace but the sword. For I have come to set a man 'against his father, a daughter against her mother, and a daughter-in-law against her mother-in-law; and one's enemies will be those of his household'" (Matthew 10:34–36).

Isn't Jesus' entire mission one of peace and love? What's with this talk of "the sword" and division within families? Although the Lord is using hyperbole to grab the listeners' attention, Jesus does intend these words to strike us deeply. If we truly live our lives as followers of Christ, we are going to ruffle some feathers. There is no reason to believe that this will not happen within our families. For instance, your husband may want to practice contraception, and you may desire to follow the teaching of the Church. What do you do? You may be longing to get married and finally meet someone who is divorced and cannot get married in the Church. Do you defy Church teaching and get married in a civil ceremony. The Lord's advice? "Whoever loves father or mother more than me is not worthy of me, and whoever loves son or daughter more than me is not worthy of me" (Matthew 10:37).

Being hated in the name of Jesus (especially by a family member) is not easy, but the reward is great. Our Lord promises that if we persevere, we will be saved. While we are always called to repay hatred with love, we cannot compromise our moral beliefs in order to please another person. Whether we encounter resistance from a known opponent or from a family member, we are expected to respond in the same manner. If we persevere and obey the Lord's commands, we are promised eternal life.

Help us to always remain faithful to you, Lord. Even when we encounter opposition from a loved one, may we always have the strength to persevere and never compromise our moral beliefs. Amen.

31.

"But rejoice to the extent that you share in the sufferings of Christ, so that when his glory is revealed you may also rejoice exultantly" (1 Peter 4:13).

Although it may not involve physical pain, being criticized or mocked because of our religious beliefs can be very painful. Most of us would do whatever we can to avoid this form of mental pain, especially when it originates from a family member or friend. As we learn more about our faith, however, we realize that all suffering has a redemptive value. Despite this fact, most of us still don't enjoy suffering. At best, we'll struggle to accept our crosses, knowing that they can be put to good use. In this Scripture verse, however, Saint Peter raises the bar. He advises us not only to accept our suffering, but to rejoice in it. Let's explore the concept further and discuss some ways that can make this seemingly impossible attitude a reality in your life.

How is it possible to rejoice over suffering? On the surface, it makes no sense. Suffering, by its very nature, is a painful experience. If we concentrate too much on the pain, however, we can easily lose sight of the big picture. In a mystical way, Jesus can use our pain to free souls, convert sinners, and assist in the redemption of all humanity. When we contrast the potential benefits with the temporary pain, it can provide us with relief and even joy. Rather than rejoicing in the actual pain associated with suffering, we are instead happy because of the long-term good that can result from our trials.

One of the people who understood this concept was Saint Thérèse of Lisieux (1873–1897). This simple Carmelite nun, known as the "Little Flower," was always seeking ways to suffer for the Lord. In her autobiography, *The Story of a Soul*, Saint Thérèse details numerous instances in which she willingly suffered in one way or another. When difficulties came her way, she would rejoice, knowing the potential value that could result from her proper handling of the situations. Every unpleasant experience encountered by Thérèse was embraced as an opportunity to unite her suffering with that of Christ. She would be an excellent person to ask for help when we struggle with our own difficulties. In her last hours, Saint Thérèse declared that her time in heaven would be dedicated to the good of those on earth. If we ask for her intercession during our times of suffering, she can help us better appreciate the value of our struggles.

Dear Saint Thérèse, please pray for us and help us to see the big picture when it comes to suffering. When we are tempted to reject our trials, remind us turn to the Lord for help in carrying our crosses. Amen.

32.

"I command you: be strong and steadfast! Do not fear nor be dismayed, for the LORD, your God, is with you wherever you go" (Joshua 1:9).

Anyone who has experienced persecution can relate to the feeling of being all alone. When facing this battle, the loneliness can become overwhelming. It should come as no surprise that one of the most popular poems for those in this situation is *Footprints in the Sand*. The idea of God walking beside us as our unseen companion can provide great comfort. This is the message spoken by the Lord to Joshua in the above Bible verse. Although he would face great opposition and danger in the Promised Land, Joshua and the Israelites would be accompanied and protected by the Lord. That same promise extends to each of us as we deal with various forms of persecution in our lives.

Several years ago, in response to a newspaper editorial criticizing Blessed Pope John Paul II, I wrote a letter defending the Holy Father and the Church's magisterium. The printed response of others to my editorial was negative, and I felt alone in my defense of the Church. As the years progressed and I embraced my Catholic faith to a greater degree, many more such occasions have arisen. Through much prayer and discernment, I have come to realize that the Lord is always with me when I defend the Church. The negative publicity of sexual abuse within the Church and the attitude of society can make it difficult to profess our faith. Invariably, when a newspaper article is published about *anything* Catholic, the reader comments always seem to involve accusations of perversion, greed, and living in the dark ages. Furthermore, this problem is not restricted to Catholics. All Christians, regardless of denomination, are met with some degree of resistance when publicly professing their faith.

Don't be discouraged! Just as the Lord promised to be with Joshua several thousand years ago, he accompanies each of us as we try to follow the Church's teachings. We are never alone in our quest to do what is right. Take comfort in the fact that God is always beside us, and threats, insults and even physical violence will never change this.

Lord, sometimes we feel like we're all alone when we try to be good. Help us to recall that you are always beside us, giving us the strength we need to persevere. Amen.

33.

"When they hand you over, do not worry about how you are to speak or what you are to say. You will be given at that moment what you are to say" (Matthew 10:19).

What is the most difficult aspect of evangelization? Many will answer that it is the inability to articulate their beliefs in a logical manner, especially when challenged. If we are in a situation where we are defending the faith, we can always count on God's help. Let's explore this Scripture passage and take a look at some implied assumptions that are associated with it.

First of all, it's incorrect to interpret Jesus' statement as meaning that we will be automatically infused with all necessary knowledge of the Catholic faith. What the Lord is promising is that we'll be given the words provided that we do our part and learn the Church's teachings. This can best be accomplished by reading the Bible, the catechism, the writings of the saints, and various official Vatican documents. If you don't like to read, we are blessed to have a number of solid Catholic resources on radio, television, and the Internet. How much time should we spend on this daily? You'd be amazed how much can be learned by devoting ten to fifteen minutes each day in dedicated study. By spending some time learning about the teachings of the Church, you'll be better prepared to deal with situations when they arise.

Even if you can't instantly rattle off Bible verses and Church doctrine, knowing where to find the information will go a long way toward helping you. It's a very good idea to build a library of reference materials and set up a series of Internet bookmarks that can be consulted when needed. When challenged about an aspect of the faith, don't feel pressured to provide an answer on the spot. Rather than make something up, it's always better to admit that you're not sure but that you'll look it up. This allows you to do the necessary research and provide a proper answer to the question.

Once we begin to put some effort into better learning the teachings of the Church, then the Lord can go to work and provide us words when necessary. There have been times when I've been amazed at what comes out of my mouth. On the other hand, I have experienced occasions when I've fallen flat on my face. When this happens, I view it as a reminder that I need to do some more study in a certain area. So, do your best to get ready for "battle" and know that the Lord will be beside you, helping defend the faith.

Grant us, O Lord, the perseverance and desire to learn more about the teachings of your Church. As a result, we'll not only get to know you better, but we'll be better prepared to defend our faith with confidence. Amen.

34.

"I have told you this so that you might have peace in me. In the world you will have trouble, but take courage, I have conquered the world" (John 16:33).

In this verse, Jesus doesn't try to sugarcoat anything. He acknowledges that we should expect trouble in our lives. However, he also tells us that "it's not that big of a deal." Huh? When we first look at the Lord's statement, it doesn't appear to make sense. As with much of what he says, however, further study proves that there is a deeper meaning to his comments.

Depending on the degree to which we practice our Christianity, we will encounter persecution. People will tolerate our religious beliefs up to a point, but we better watch out when we cross the line. Christianity and persecution go hand in hand. Although it may be painful, suffering for our religious beliefs is usually a sign that we're doing a good job. I once heard a priest state that if we didn't experience some form of persecution, we probably weren't practicing our faith as much as we should.

While the negative aspects of religious persecution are obvious, we shouldn't forget that there is a benefit to suffering for the faith. In his Sermon on the Mount, Jesus pointed out the benefits of religious persecution:

Blessed are they who are persecuted for the sake of righteousness, for theirs is the kingdom of heaven. Blessed are you when they insult you and persecute you and utter every kind of evil against you [falsely] because of me. Rejoice and be glad, for your reward will be great in heaven. Thus they persecuted the prophets who were before you.

MATTHEW 5:10–12

When we read the Lord's comments, we will notice and be comforted that Christ is comparing us to the prophets, who were persecuted for sharing their faith. That's pretty good company! Even more reassuring is his promise that, by suffering in this way, we will receive a great reward in heaven. By meditating on these words, we can begin to feel the Lord's peace descend upon us. What previously seemed paradoxical suddenly begins to make sense. Although we may have to undergo temporary suffering, the end result will make it worthwhile.

Lord, help us to overcome the fear of religious persecution by recalling your words in the Beatitudes. May we always stand firm, knowing that a great reward awaits us in heaven. Amen.

35.

"I shall show you whom to fear. Be afraid of the one who after killing has the power to cast into Gehenna; yes, I tell you, be afraid of that one" (Luke 12:5).

Some people are not going to be happy that we are practicing Catholics, especially if we try to share our faith with them. We may be mocked, threatened, assaulted, or even murdered in certain circumstances. In each of these situations, the Lord's message is the same—do not be afraid! Even though it may involve a great deal of suffering on earth, our reward in heaven will be great. Given that, the last thing you would expect to hear from the Lord is that there is someone of whom we *should* be afraid. Even more surprising is the fact that I'd include it in a book designed to provide freedom from worry. Lo and behold, here we have Jesus pointing out an exception to the rule. And it is an exception that we should all take *very* seriously!

Let's discuss the good news first. No matter how seriously we may be attacked for our beliefs, any damage inflicted upon us is only temporary. When discussing the reality of religious persecution, Jesus makes the following statement: "I tell you, my friends, do not be afraid of those who kill the body but after that can do no more" (Luke 12:4).

Even if we lose our faith, our eternal salvation cannot be taken away. In fact, those who give up their lives in defense of the Lord are known as martyrs, and their salvation is assured. While most of us will not endure physical suffering for our religious beliefs, we should be comforted with this promise, as it obviously covers verbal abuse as well. Although it may not feel good while we are experiencing the persecution, we can persevere, knowing that there is a limit to the damage that can be inflicted.

What about the one who "has the power to cast into Gehenna," the individual of whom we should be afraid? That unsavory character is known as Satan, and he can be a very real threat to our salvation. Although the Church teaches that (contrary to comedian Flip Wilson's old catch phrase) the devil can't *make* us do anything, he certainly can trick us into sinning. He can use an endless stream of lies and deceptions to convince us to turn away from God. Unfortunately, in today's world many people refuse to believe in his existence. Having that attitude allows us to become easy prey, as we can be caught unaware. Cognizant of this threat, Saint Peter issued the following stern warning: "Be sober and vigilant. Your opponent the devil is prowling around like a roaring lion looking for [someone] to devour" (1 Peter 5:8).

How does the evil one tempt us? Not by dressing up in a red suit and carrying a pitchfork, as we see in the old cartoons. Instead, he makes sin look attractive and appealing. The suggestive picture found on the Internet, the temptation to save money by illegally downloading music or the desire to "curse out" the driver who just cut us off may seem appealing at the time, but they can lead to our spiritual downfall. Although the purpose of this book is to free you from anxiety, never forget that a good healthy awareness of the devil's deceit is essential. By remaining on your toes, you'll be able to thwart his efforts to take away your eternal happiness.

Help us, O Lord, to be sober and vigilant in order to resist Satan and his lies. Through prayer and frequent reception of the sacraments, may we always remain under your protection. Amen.

CHAPTER 6

Sickness

Despite having no major health problems, my friend, Lou, was always afraid that he would get cancer. He was diligent about routine medical examinations but always feared he'd one day receive the dreaded "Big C" diagnosis. That day did indeed come, and Lou was told he had cancer. His greatest fear had become a reality. After years of worrying that he wouldn't be able to endure the physical and mental suffering associated with the disease, he was about to find out for sure. Surprisingly for Lou, but not for those of us who knew him well, he did fine. His strong faith, including a devotion to the Blessed Mother, allowed him to maintain a sense of peace throughout the ordeal. Even though he was in a great deal of pain, he was still able to experience peacefulness. He maintained a sense of optimism and acceptance even when faced with multiple sets of grim test results. After struggling valiantly for several months, Lou passed away. According to his sister, Sherry, Lou appeared to have a slight smile on his face when he died.

Nothing can put our faith to the test as much as serious illness. Facing this situation can easily derail our prayer life and even cause us to lose all hope. Turning to the Bible, however, helps us to see things in a different light. Instead of gloom and despair, we see numerous stories of healing and peace. In several instances, Jesus granted miraculous physical healings and can still do so today. I have witnessed this personally with my daughters, Mary and Elizabeth, who were not expected to be born alive. In other cases, God grants spiritual healings which are often accompanied by great peace. Rather than being a curse, sickness can be a blessing. It can provide us with an opportunity to trust in the Lord and even allow us to experience a supernatural peace, greater than any comfort the world can provide.

36.

"On hearing this, Jesus answered him, 'Do not be afraid; just have faith and she will be saved'" (Luke 8:50).

Wouldn't it be great if we could have lived in the Middle East two thousand years ago, when Jesus walked the earth preaching and performing miracles? We could consult him with our problems and ask him to heal our infirmities. People back then had it so much easier because they didn't have to rely on all of this "faith" business. If we could actually see Jesus cure someone, it would be much easier to trust his ability to do so in our own lives. While we all may be tempted to feel this way sometimes, the answer isn't quite that simple. This can be seen by looking at an incident that took place during Jesus' public ministry.

When the twelve-year-old daughter of Jairus (a synagogue official) was dying, he knelt before Jesus and asked him to come to his house. In the meantime, someone arrived and announced that the girl had died. Bad timing...should have acted on it sooner...end of story, right? Not a chance! Our Lord responded with the above words, indicating that it was still not too late. Jesus journeyed to the house of Jairus and repeated his assertion that the girl was not dead. In what can be viewed as a great indication that human nature hasn't changed much in two thousand years, Saint Luke writes: "And they ridiculed him, because they knew that she was dead" (Luke 8:53).

If we back up a few verses, we see that while Jesus was speaking to Jairus, he paused to heal a woman who had been suffering from hemorrhages for twelve years (Luke 8:43–48). Surely, word of this would have reached some of those who were at the house. Yet they still ridiculed Jesus because they felt there was no hope. Hard to believe, isn't it?

As this incident illustrates, there has never been a shortage of individuals who try to take away one's hope in a difficult situation. Claiming to be realistic, they present a list of reasons why the answer to a prayer won't be granted. When ridiculed as he arrived at the home of Jairus, the Lord ignored the insults and proceeded to heal the young girl. The Bible makes no mention of how the people react, but I wouldn't be at all surprised if they went on to explain away the healing as being some sort of fluke. Even when confronted with a miracle, some folks will find a way to deny that it actually took place.

What can we learn from this? To put it simply, Jesus can heal any medical condition we encounter. Don't let anyone try to tell you otherwise. Will he always provide a physical healing? No. As hard as it is for us to understand, sometimes that healing is not what's best for us or our loved ones. As our faith in God increases, however, we will learn to accept that whatever happens is in our best interest. While it may not happen overnight, working toward having this attitude is the secret to achieving peace.

....

Lord, help us believe that you can still perform miracles. Let us never cease praying for miraculous healings, accepting the answer that you provide. Amen.

....

37.

"No trial has come to you but what is human. God is faithful and will not let you be tried beyond your strength; but with the trial he will also provide a way out, so that you may be able to bear it" (1 Corinthians 10:13).

As an anxiety-prone individual, I constantly have to fight off the urge to worry about potential problems. Many of us have a list of "what ifs" that can cause us to spend time worrying. These "yet-to-occur" difficulties can result in sleepless nights or physical ailments:

What if I lose my job?
What if my spouse dies?
What if my car breaks down?
What if I fail at homeschooling my children?
What if....

One of the most common *what ifs* is the fear of getting a serious illness. Many of us determine, in advance, that we won't be able to handle the suffering that goes along with a prolonged illness. Depending on how worry-prone we are, this imaginary ailment can cause us to become paralyzed with fear. As someone who's been there, I can assure you that this type of anxiety is completely useless and counterproductive. Furthermore, this kind of thinking can be overcome.

We must always remember that God does not give us grace to deal with imaginary problems. The reason that these "problems" are so insurmountable is precisely because they are not real. Just as the test of the Emergency Broadcast System reminds us that "if this had been an actual emergency...," we can hear the Lord saying, "If this had been an actual problem, you would have been given the grace to deal with it." That is Saint Paul's message to the people of Corinth and each of us. If you are asked to endure a serious problem, such as sickness, you will be given the necessary grace to persevere.

Those of us who have experienced a life-threatening illness realize that there is a sense of peace that descends upon us when we ask the Lord for help. Of course, we can reject this peace and choose to let our minds run wild with anxious thoughts, but that is not God's fault. We have been given free will and can choose to worry instead of accepting the gift of peace.

Rest assured of one thing: If the Lord permits you to be stricken with a serious illness, such as cancer, you *will* be able to bear it. That is God's promise to you, as delivered by the pen of Saint Paul. That message should be sufficient to allay your fears about the future. If not, keep reading and meditating upon this verse. When you need God's grace, it will be there.

Help us trust in your will for our lives, Lord. When we are asked to carry a heavy cross, allow us to remember that you will always give us the necessary grace. Amen.

38.

"So you also are now in anguish. But I will see you again, and your hearts will rejoice, and no one will take your joy away from you" (John 16:22).

Several years ago, I was a computer programmer and was very comfortable with my job. One day, without any warning, I was suddenly assigned the task of providing telephone support for a completely unfamiliar software package. Unfortunately, the people I was helping knew a lot more about the product than I did. In an effort to relieve my stress, my new supervisor assured me that "nothing lasts forever at this company." That simple comment provided me with hope that this assignment was only temporary and that it was not the end of the world. I was now able to deal with the new situation because I knew it wasn't permanent.

Suffering is always easier to bear when there is an end in sight. Not being able to see the finish line multiplies the severity of our pain. When we are in the midst of a prolonged illness, it's easy to feel as if things will never improve. When we look at Jesus' words above, however, we are reassured that all pain and suffering will come to an end one day. Even if our agony is not relieved in this life, it will cease to be in the next. Originally addressed to the apostles at the Last Supper, this verse speaks to the anguish that will descend upon them in the coming days. While acknowledging the suffering that will take place due to his impending death, Jesus calls attention to the eternal joy that awaits them in the future.

That same message is addressed to anyone who is battling an illness or in need of hope. More than just a sentimental greeting-card message, the Lord's words give us a life preserver in a sea of uncertainty. Jesus' words can allow us to willingly accept our cross, knowing that it will one day be taken away. In what may seem like a radical move, I suggest that we thank God for our suffering and treat it as a gift. Even though having that mindset doesn't remove our physical pain, it does help to reorient our thinking. When we unite our pain with that of Christ, we are able to share in his mission.

Looking at suffering as a gift is not something that comes naturally and is an acquired skill. Frequent prayer and reading the Bible will better equip us to adopt this position. When suffering from an illness, our instinct is to view it as a misfortune. With the Lord's help, however, we can better see the bigger picture and know that tremendous good can result from our illness. Coupled with the reminder that all suffering is temporary, we can better carry our cross, following Christ's example.

> *Jesus, when all is dark in our lives, help us to remember that our suffering will one day end. Until it does, infuse us with the grace necessary to carry our cross. For, in doing so, we know that infinite good can result. Amen.*

39.

"A large number of people from the towns in the vicinity of Jerusalem also gathered, bringing the sick and those disturbed by unclean spirits, and they were all cured" (Acts 5:16).

After Jesus ascended into heaven, the apostles carried on his work. One of the practices that they continued was the healing of the sick. Scripture tells us that many people were healed as a result of their efforts (Acts 5:12–16). While the healings took place at the hand of the apostles, the actual power to heal emanated from Christ. One can only imagine how excited everyone must have been to witness such miraculous events. Well, not exactly everyone. If we continue reading, we'll see the reward that the apostles received for their work. Fueled by jealousy, the high priest and the Sadducees threw them in jail. Fortunately, an angel intervened and allowed them to escape (Acts 5:19). The apostles then went right back to their work of proclaiming the Good News.

What can we learn from this situation? For one thing, we can take comfort in the Lord's ability to perform physical or spiritual healings. Even though he had already ascended into heaven, his healing power remained and was channeled through the apostles. Now that the apostles have passed on, do we miss out on this type of healing? Fortunately for us, we can access this same healing power through the anointing of the sick. Documented in the Bible (James 5:14–15), this powerful outpouring of the Lord's grace can fortify those facing serious illness. According to the *Catechism of the Catholic Church*, the special graces associated with this sacrament are:

> the uniting of the sick person to the passion of Christ, for his own good and that of the whole Church;
>
> the strengthening, peace, and courage to endure in a Christian manner the sufferings of illness or old age;
>
> the forgiveness of sins, if the sick person was not able to obtain it through the sacrament of Penance;
>
> the restoration of health, if it is conducive to the salvation of his soul;
>
> the preparation for passing over to eternal life. (CCC 1532)

It's comforting to know that, in addition to our own ability to pray for healing, the Church offers a supernatural infusion of healing through the sacrament of anointing of the sick. Although the reception of this sacrament does not guarantee the restoration of one's health, there are many benefits associated with it. When dealing with a serious illness, every effort should be made to receive this anointing, even if the illness is not terminal. Anointing is for the *sick*, not simply for those whose cause is more dire. For example, many cancers today can be cured through surgery by early detection, but are not these individuals still in need of the Lord's grace? The Lord desires us to ask for healing graces when we are most in need.

Thank you, Lord, for the gift of the anointing of the sick. May we always avail ourselves of this sacrament when needed, knowing the graces provided will ease the burden imposed by illness. Amen.

40.

"Jesus turned around and saw her, and said, 'Courage, daughter! Your faith has saved you.' And from that hour the woman was cured" *(Matthew 9:22).*

Looking at this verse, two words come to mind—persistence and faith. This woman was suffering from hemorrhages for twelve years but never gave up hope. Moreover, her faith in Jesus was so strong that she knew her cure would come just by touching his cloak (Matthew 9:21). As if suffering from this condition wasn't bad enough, the nature of the ailment caused her to be shunned and viewed as unclean. Despite all of the odds being against her, however, she went for it and approached Jesus for healing. As a result, her request was granted.

When we look at the details of this case, we see a woman who had every reason to be pessimistic about ever being cured. We can all become so overwhelmed with the hopelessness of our situation that we make the mistake of ceasing to pray. The medical facts and statistics can blind us to the fact that Jesus is the ultimate physician and can cure any ailment. While I'm not recommending an unrealistic view toward medical issues, I am advocating that we recall the Lord's ability to cure any disease. Please remember that, no matter how grim a diagnosis you or your loved one receives, there is *always* hope.

Another lesson illustrated by this encounter is the importance of being persistent in prayer. Despite twelve years of illness, the woman never stopped seeking a cure. In the parable of the Persistent Widow (Luke 18:1–14), an unjust judge is repeatedly asked by the widow to render a decision in her favor. Eventually he gives in and does as she wishes. What is the point of the story? Saint Luke is very clear: "Then he told them a parable about the necessity for them to pray always without becoming weary" (Luke 18:1).

If we have a need in our lives, we should keep praying and not become discouraged. Whenever I'm asked to pray for someone who is sick, I never hesitate to pray for a complete physical healing, BUT I always submit to the Lord's will, as God knows what is best for that individual. When my father was diagnosed with cancer, I prayed for him to be healed even though the odds were not in his favor. When he died just one month later, that healing took place and the cancer was gone. Although it wasn't the healing I had in mind, it was the one he needed.

Lord, help us to remain persistent as we present our needs to you. However, please increase our faith so that we can better accept your answer, knowing that your will is perfect. Amen.

41.

"Now I rejoice in my sufferings for your sake, and in my flesh I am filling up what is lacking in the afflictions of Christ on behalf of his body, which is the church" (Colossians 1:24).

What do you find more confusing about this statement: the fact that Saint Paul is rejoicing because of his suffering or his assertion that Christ's suffering was somehow incomplete? This is one of those verses that novice Bible readers love to skip over, due to the fact that it's so confusing. When it comes to dealing with difficulties, however, this verse arguably explains the value of redemptive suffering better than any other. Most Catholics are familiar with the words, *offer it up*, but let's delve into the meaning of this important saying.

In order to prevent any major confusion, let's clear up one thing. Jesus' sacrifice on the cross was completely sufficient for our redemption. There is absolutely nothing lacking in the Lord's passion, death, and resurrection. He did exactly what was necessary to open the gates of heaven for us. Any interpretation of this verse that assumes otherwise is simply incorrect. That being the case, what exactly is Saint Paul talking about when he refers to Christ's afflictions as lacking? In his encyclical on the Mystical Body of Christ (*Mystici Corporis Christi*), Pope Pius XII shares some insightful observations, asserting that God wills that the body of Christ participates in the salvific act of Jesus. Through prayer and penance according to the encyclical, the people of God mystically cooperate in the saving work of Jesus.

Meditating upon this concept helps us understand just how it is possible to rejoice in one's suffering. Although it may not remove the pain, we can feel privileged to participate through our suffering in the Lord's mission. How and why it works is not as important as the fact that it *does* work. In his infinite wisdom and goodness, Jesus entrusts us with a very important task—bringing new meaning to the phrase *offer it up*. If you are struggling with an illness and find it difficult to pray, your malady can become your prayer. When offered to the Lord, this prayer can have unlimited benefits. That should be more than enough to make us rejoice.

Help us to always unite our suffering with yours, Lord. Even when we find ourselves unable to speak the words of prayer, let our unspoken prayers of suffering be pleasing to you. Amen.

42.

"When Jesus saw her, he called to her and said, 'Woman, you are set free of your infirmity.' He laid his hands on her, and she at once stood up straight and glorified God"(Luke 13:12–13).

Imagine being sick for eighteen years without an end in sight. It's quite possible that some of you may be in a similar position and can relate to the angst experienced by the woman in the above passage. Despite the fact that she was bent over and couldn't stand erect, she journeyed to the synagogue to hear Jesus teach. When Jesus laid hands on her, the woman was healed, stood up and glorified God. What a tremendous sight that must have been! This woman, who had previously been unable to stand up straight, was now standing erect and praising God. Do you know what I really like about this story? Jesus reached out and touched someone who was suffering and, as a result, she was better able to give praise. In other words, his touch drew her closer to him. This same type of healing can happen to anyone who is sick and who desires to grow closer to Christ.

Although the details of this narrative appear to suggest that Jesus initiated the contact, it's important to note that the woman was *in* the synagogue. In obedience to God's commandment to "keep holy the Lord's day," she journeyed to the synagogue on the Sabbath. By doing so, she was able to experience Jesus' healing touch. Even though she was stricken with a debilitating ailment, she took the necessary steps to be in God's proximity.

The lesson we can learn from this is that, no matter what our circumstances, we should make an effort to place ourselves in the Lord's presence. This can be done even if we're too sick to get out of bed. We can accomplish this through prayer, reading the Bible, watching spiritual programs on television, or listening to them on the radio. This enables anyone to be in the Lord's presence, albeit in a nontraditional way. Most importantly, we can also arrange for the reception of the Eucharist from a priest or extraordinary minister of holy Communion.

Placing ourselves in the Lord's presence will make things happen. Although we are not guaranteed a physical healing, we can be confident that we'll receive what we need. Then, like the woman in the story, we can glorify and praise the Lord to the fullest extent possible.

....

Lord, just like the woman who patiently accepted her eighteen years of suffering, help us remain hopeful and continually turn to you. By doing so, we know we will receive the healing we need. Amen.

....

CHAPTER 7:

Trials and Tribulations

One of life's greatest challenges is maintaining a sense of composure when faced with trials and tribulations. Being a Christian should make this easier, but we often get so overwhelmed that this advantage is nullified. In order to achieve a sense of peace during trials, we must stay close to the Lord. While we may be able to get by on our own temporarily, we'll eventually reach our breaking point. Positive thinking will only get us so far. In order to persevere as we are pounded by the storms of life, the Lord's grace is needed.

When I was a college student, I joined a Catholic prayer group. Led by two priests, this large group comprised lay people of various ages. The common characteristic of those involved was a strong belief in God's providence. No matter what tragedy or difficulty these people were faced with, the response was the same. Death, unemployment, illness, or any other imaginable problem all brought about the response of..."Praise God!" While I desperately wanted to share in their practice of giving thanks in all circumstances, part of me felt that they were out of touch with reality. To make matters worse, whenever I tried to put their *no worries* philosophy into practice outside the group, there was never a shortage of people who would remind me that I wasn't being realistic.

As I've grown closer to the Lord, I now realize that the folks in the prayer group were completely correct. God doesn't want us to worry needlessly and can help us to trust in all circumstances. How is this possible? Rather than by consulting the experts of the world, let's start by opening up the Bible. By doing so, we'll be able to hear the Lord urge us to trust in *all* circumstances—good and bad!

43.

"Come to me, all you who labor and are burdened, and I will give you rest" (Matthew 11:28).

In 1997, my wife Eileen was pregnant with our twin daughters. A few months into the pregnancy, the girls were diagnosed with a life-threatening ailment known as twin-to-twin transfusion syndrome. According to the doctors, our children had very little chance of being born alive. Despite the grim prognosis, Eileen and I journeyed to Our Lady of Lourdes Hospital in Camden, New Jersey, two times a week for a procedure that eliminated excess amniotic fluid surrounding the girls. Although this was a long-shot treatment, the fact that we were doing something gave us hope. After each appointment, we'd make our way to the beautiful and traditional hospital chapel. Eileen and I would kneel before the Lord, present in the tabernacle, and plead for Mary and Elizabeth to be healed. Above the altar, just below the ceiling, was the Bible verse at the top of this page. Although we were very much burdened, my eyes would glance at Jesus' words and I would feel a sense of peace. Even though the odds were not good and the future was unknown, I felt something happen. For a moment, I was at peace.

When we find ourselves consumed by worry and fear, we often blame the Lord for failing to follow through on promises. Sometimes we feel that the only way we'll experience peace is by the elimination of our problems. Instead of asking for God's help to bear our burden, we narrow-mindedly focus on the fact that the problem still exists. We forget that the Lord's promise of peace is not contingent upon the disappearance of our problems.

As I write this, my twins are healthy fourteen-year-old girls. Although the burden caused by their medical condition is now gone, it has been replaced by other potential sources of anxiety. Our Lord's words to me are still as pertinent today as they were when I knelt in that chapel. God invites me to come daily and obtain the rest I need. In the same way, the Lord is calling you. Rather than being a promise of a problem-free life, the words of Jesus assure us of a heavenly peace even in the midst of turmoil. Are you burdened? Do you find yourself in need of rest? Jesus is waiting for you in the sacrament of the Eucharist, he sits in the confessional ready to forgive your sins, he is prepared to speak to you when you open up the Bible. Don't pass up the chance. Turn to Christ today.

Sweet Jesus, we are burdened and weary. We turn to you this day and ask for the graces needed to carry our crosses without fear. Please grant us the rest and peace that come along with being your disciples. Amen.

44.

"The Lord said to her in reply, 'Martha, Martha, you are anxious and worried about many things. There is need of only one thing. Mary has chosen the better part and it will not be taken from her'" (Luke 10:41–42).

The saga of Martha and Mary (Luke 10:38–42) sometimes raises more questions than answers. We are told that these two sisters behaved quite differently in the presence of the Lord. As Martha rushed around and waited on Jesus, Mary sat at his feet and listened to him speak. Frustrated and exhausted, Martha finally turned to Jesus and exclaimed, "Lord, do you not care that my sister has left me by myself to do the serving? Tell her to help me." Much to Martha's chagrin, the Lord responded with the words in Luke 10:41–42. The age-old question is: who's right, Martha or Mary?

While Jesus acknowledged that "Mary has chosen the better part," he never said that Martha was wrong. What is the Lord trying to say and what can we learn from this statement? Scholars have always viewed this encounter as representing the conflict between the active and the contemplative life. Even though Jesus did state that Mary's approach was better, we would be wise to incorporate some of both Martha and Mary's behavior into our lives.

Possibly the best lesson that we can learn from this story is the importance of balance in our lives. If we attempt to worship God solely by our actions in church, our relationship with the Lord will be lacking. As Christians, we need to find a way to meet God everywhere. While that obviously includes worshiping at church, it also means that we must strive to see God in our coworkers, angry customers, or drivers trying to cut us off in traffic. Quite a challenge, right? Yes, but it is possible to achieve this balance by using the right approach.

Saint Paul teaches us to "pray without ceasing" (1 Thessalonians 5:17), and this seemingly unachievable command is further proof that we can integrate the contemplative and active aspects of our lives. How can we pray constantly if we have other duties? We can do this by offering all of our actions throughout the day to the Lord. If we make this offering in the morning, the rest of our day can be spent praising God in all we do. Whether we use a traditional Morning Offering prayer or our own words, the basic idea is the same. All of the day's activities become a prayer.

When the crises and trials come, we can use this approach to weather the storm. Early in the day, before things get too hectic, we can make this powerful offering and thus combine the approaches of Martha and Mary. As time permits throughout the day, we should also try to make some time to converse with the Lord through prayer. By using this approach, we can rest assured that we're effectively using both the Martha and the Mary approach to our faith.

We offer you everything that we do today, Lord. Please accept the offering of our works and use them as you see fit. Amen.

45.

"Think of what is above, not of what is on earth" (Colossians 3:2).

In my younger days, I would use a fairly common technique to deal with unpleasant situations. When forced to do something uncomfortable, I would always plan to do something pleasant afterward. That would enable me to look past the anxiety-producing activity and focus on the reward. If I had to give a presentation in class, I would plan to buy a new comic book or magazine. If I had to get a medical test, I would plan to go out for junk food afterward. Although the rewards weren't elaborate, they enabled me to divert my attention from what was frightening me and gave me a ray of hope. Although I still practice this technique, I have learned to rely more on prayer, spiritual reading, and the sacraments to provide comfort.

In our life on earth, it is inevitable that we will encounter many difficulties. Before we leave this world, we'll all experience our share of flat tires, medical emergencies, and personal tragedies. As followers of Christ, however, we understand the necessity of these burdens. As stated earlier in this book, this life is not intended to be a problem-free paradise. I once heard a priest proclaim that "Jesus never said, come join the party!" Instead, he promised us daily crosses (Luke 9:23) in this life and the possibility of eternal happiness in the next. Given that fact, we must constantly keep our eye on the Lord. If we concentrate too much on our trials and tribulations, we can easily get beaten down and end up straying from the path that leads to heaven.

I agree that it's often difficult to put this into practice. When we're dealing with adversity on a daily basis, it's difficult *not* to focus on our problems. One simple trick that works for me was suggested by my friend, Michelle. She shared that whenever she saw the sun, she thought of *the Son*. The rays of sunlight represent his love for each of us. Although it sounds simple, it really works for me. I can't tell you how many times I've been driving in the car, worrying about something, when I see the sun and recall Christ's love for me. Before long, I find myself thinking less about my problems and more about God's providence in my life. I begin to speak with the Lord instead of worrying, and my sense of peace is restored. Suddenly, I've gone from worrying to praying.

Lord, when all we can focus on is our troubles, help us to glance heavenward and concentrate on you instead. As a result, allow your peace to descend on us like golden rays of sunshine. Amen.

46.

"He said to [his] disciples, 'Therefore I tell you, do not worry about your life and what you will eat, or about your body and what you will wear'" (Luke 12:22).

Try telling this to people who are unemployed and struggling to pay their monthly bills and there is a good chance that you'll get an earful. While most financially challenged people would view this as a difficult pill to swallow, it can actually be a great source of comfort when meditated upon, and here is why. This message is coming directly from Jesus. These are his words and they mean something. Like a parent who responds to a child's "why?" with, "Because I said so," the Lord is telling us not to worry about these things. And looking at this realistically, doesn't it make sense that the Lord knows best? Even though it seems counterintuitive, let's look at why Jesus' advice is solid and how it can be followed.

Obviously, if Jesus tells us not to worry, then we should take his words at face value. Human nature being what it is, however, makes this a difficult task. What may help to convince us is a question that he raises a few verses later: "Can any of you by worrying add a moment to your lifespan?" (Luke 12:25).

One thing that can be said about worry is that it's useless. Why is it that we spend so much time doing something useless? The reason is most likely due to a combination of our temperament and the underestimation of God's providence. Some people, like yours truly, are hard-wired to worry. It's almost instinctive that as soon as problems arise, the worrying kicks in. In spite of this, we can learn to modify our behavior and use our energy productively.

What are some productive activities we can undertake when faced with problems? Prayer, reading the Bible, and receiving the sacraments will all produce positive results in our lives. Suppose, for instance, that you suddenly lost your job today. I guarantee that if you took your Bible and read the above verses several times throughout the day you would feel some sense of peace. Now, you might have to read them lots of times for a few days before the peace sets in, but the feeling would eventually arrive. Why? Because the Lord is speaking directly to you through the pages of the Bible, and they really do have an effect. Additionally, your prayers may result in a new and better job. I can guarantee that worrying won't yield the same positive results.

Lord Jesus, help us to take your words seriously and turn to you in times of need. By doing so, we will experience peace and receive the grace that will assist us in dealing with our trials. Amen.

47.

"Consider it all joy, my brothers, when you encounter various trials, for you know that the testing of your faith produces perseverance" (James 1:2–3).

When undergoing trials and tribulations, one of the secrets to remaining peaceful is learning to appreciate the value of these difficulties. Obviously, this outlook does not come naturally. We've learned from an early age that if something is painful, it should be avoided. This response is so instinctive that it's even understood by animals. My dog, Gracie, hates to be brushed. As a result, she now runs away when she sees the brush. In the same way, we have a tendency to avoid painful situations in our lives. Why? Because they're painful! If we're looking to achieve peace in our lives, however, we must somehow learn to see the value in our problems.

In his letter, Saint James emphasizes the value of trials. Over time, the proper handling of difficult issues toughens us up and helps to diminish our tendency to be controlled by our feelings. I was always amazed by the strength of my wife's grandmother in times of adversity. When I asked my mother-in-law about this, she told me, "Nana's been through a lot." It's hard to disagree as she lost her husband, her son, and her son-in-law at relatively young ages. While enduring these trials, Nana turned to the Lord for help. As a result, her faith grew and she learned to trust in God's providence. As each new situation presented itself, she knew that the Lord would help her to endure. Hence, the suffering made her a stronger and more peaceful person.

As Christians, there is another benefit to experiencing difficulties in our lives. Properly responding to these trials can yield great fruit. If we grumble or feel sorry for ourselves when bad luck comes our way, we completely waste the redemptive value of our suffering. On the other hand, if we unite our suffering with the Lord's and offer it up, these tribulations can be used for the advancement of God's kingdom. In laymen's terms, this means that people can get to heaven because we offer up our suffering. This fact really hits home when we throw in the fact that one of those people who may get to heaven is *you*.

When we look at the positive value of suffering, we can understand why Saint James wrote what he did. Initially, we may not be able to consider it all joy when we encounter trials, but that outlook can develop over time. It will not happen, however, if we choose to drown our sorrows through distractions such as shopping and alcohol. Instead, we must turn to God when the storms arrive. Time spent complaining or running from our problems is wasted, but time spent praying or reading the Bible always produces results. Even though your problems may not disappear, you will be at peace and know that offering up your trials will help many people—enough to turn sorrow into joy.

....

Lord, help us to be thankful for the trials in our lives. When we are tempted to lash out and feel sorry for ourselves, remind us to turn to you for help in carrying our crosses. Amen.

....

48.

"Rejoice always. Pray without ceasing. In all circumstances give thanks, for this is the will of God for you in Christ Jesus" (1 Thessalonians 5:16–18).

If you are experiencing difficulties in your life, the above words of Saint Paul may be the last thing you want to hear. If we take a step back and look at these words objectively, however, a very comforting message begins to emerge. When uncontrollable events take place in our lives, we can rejoice (or at least try not to complain), knowing that it is happening for our own good. By doing so, we will be living according to the familiar words in the Lord's Prayer: *thy will be done.*

We repeat this phrase every time we pray the Our Father, but are we sincere? When difficulties arise in our lives, we often abandon the *thy will be done* approach and adopt the *my will be done* philosophy. Since the Lord's Prayer comes directly from Jesus, he must want us to mean the words that we say. Therefore, let's explore the idea of embracing God's will, even if it's not always pleasant.

We should pursue the desire to follow God's will. Even though it sounds simple, this can be difficult. Since it may involve inconvenience or suffering, we are sometimes reluctant to subscribe to God's plan. We'd rather follow our own plan, involving less pain and suffering. When we pray, however, we should instead strive to imitate the words spoken by Jesus in the Garden of Gethsemane: "My Father, if it is possible, let this cup pass from me; yet, not as I will, but as you will" (Matthew 26:39).

Using Christ's prayer as an example, we should never hesitate to pray for our needs. However, we must always be willing to accept the Father's decision. When we think about this logically, it makes perfect sense as God only wills what is best for us. Jesus confirmed this with the following words: "If you then, who are wicked, know how to give good gifts to your children, how much more will your heavenly Father give good things to those who ask him" (Matthew 7:11).

No matter what happens in our lives (good or bad), we should give thanks. If our prayers don't get answered in the way we expect, we should still give thanks. Why? Whether we like it or not, God sometimes permits unpleasant events to occur. Looking at Saint Paul's message, we can rest assured that these things happen because they're good for our eternal salvation. By embracing these events and offering up any corresponding suffering, we can be confident that we are not just *saying thy will be done,* but *living* it.

Help us, Lord, to echo your words to the Father as you said:
Thy will be done. Increase our desire to submit to your will in all
circumstances, even when they are painful. Amen.

49.

"They came and woke him saying, 'Master, master, we are perishing!'
He awakened, rebuked the wind and the waves, and they subsided and
there was a calm" (Luke 8:24).

Before I started to drive, my parents signed me up for a driver's education course. The curriculum consisted of a combination of classroom lectures and actual time driving on the road. We learned all of the basics necessary to operate a motor vehicle. The subject matter included lessons on safe following distance, how to handle emergencies (such as failing brakes), and the proper way to grip a steering wheel. One topic that was addressed in great detail was how to maintain control of the car while skidding on ice. We were taught to turn into the skid and accelerate slightly. Through a series of diagrams and explanations, the instructor gave us the guidelines needed to handle this dangerous situation. Since this course took place during the summer, I never got to practice this technique on the road. I knew the rules, however, so I felt prepared to handle the situation should it arise.

A few years later, I was driving down a snowy road when I got the opportunity to put my knowledge into practice. As my car began to skid, however, I never even thought about the advice to *turn into the skid and accelerate slightly.* Instead, I let my instincts take over and I turned away from the skid and slammed on the brake! The car started to spin and I turned the wheel the other way in a frantic attempt to regain control. As a result, I was now doing a complete 360 on a busy street. Fortunately for me, there were no other cars around and I eventually came to a stop with no damage to the car. I learned an important lesson that day. Knowing the facts and putting them into practice are two very different things.

This same principle applies to our spiritual lives. It is important to read the Bible and other spiritual books in order to learn what God expects from us, but we must then put this knowledge into practice. In Luke's Gospel, we see that the apostles witnessed healings (Luke 7:1–10), the raising of a man from the dead (Luke 7:11–17), and they learned many lessons from Jesus' parables (Luke 8:4–18). When surrounded by a storm at sea (Luke 8:22–15), however, everything went out the window and they panicked. This is exactly what happened to me on the icy road and what often happens to us when threatened by the problems of life. This book contains fifty Bible verses that can help us control anxiety, but only if we put them into action. We must find a way to use God's words to deal with our everyday storms. How can we do so? By lots of prayer and frequent Bible reading, which allows us to recall God's words.

Over time, fortified by an increased knowledge of the Bible and the Lord's providence, we'll find ourselves reacting differently to problems in our lives. Whereas previously our instinct may have been to panic, we'll soon have the presence of mind to say a prayer first and trust that God knows what's best. This process can take time, especially since many of us have gotten so used to panicking. The Lord understands this and will patiently guide us as we try to change our behavior. Never give up....The effort will result in your anxiety being replaced with peace.

Lord, help us to always turn to you when things go wrong. Give us the perseverance to pray and meditate on your words in sacred Scripture so that we will have an increased trust in your divine providence. Amen.

CHAPTER 8

The Secret Weapon

50.

"Then he said to the disciple, 'Behold, your mother.' And from that hour the disciple took her into his home" (John 19:27).

There are many verses in the Bible that can help to ease our anxieties. I have selected fifty key verses for this book, but in reality there are hundreds, even thousands of verses that can reassure us in times of need. It can be argued that *every* verse in the Bible can be used as a comfort when we are weary. For when we open the pages of sacred Scripture, we can hear God speak directly to us with a clear message. No matter how bad things get for us on earth, there is always hope. One day, our troubles will cease and we can look forward to the promise of eternal life in heaven. In the meantime, however, we must find a way to deal with our problems so that our eternal reward will become a reality. Fortunately, the Lord has given us a priceless gift to assist us. I like to refer to that gift as *the secret weapon*.

In many ways, our lives can be compared to the wedding at Cana (John 2:1–12). We are often cruising along, without a worry in the world when...the wine runs dry! Our lives, just like the wedding celebration, can suddenly be disrupted by an unexpected problem. Back in our Lord's time, running out of wine at a wedding was a BIG problem. In our lives, being laid off or being diagnosed with cancer are also big problems. Despite these serious issues, we are never alone. There was someone present at the wedding in Cana who is also with us, watching over our shoulders. That person, who first noticed the shortage of wine and who likewise notices the issues in our lives, is our Blessed Mother, Mary.

Some may question Mary's importance at the wedding, but Saint John's introductory comments prove otherwise: "On the third day there was a wedding in Cana in Galilee, and the mother of Jesus was there. Jesus and his disciples were also invited to the wedding" (John 2:1-2).

What is striking about this passage is the order in which the guests are listed. Isn't it odd that Jesus is about to perform his first miracle, yet Mary is introduced first? Anyone familiar with Saint John's writing style knows that he pays great attention to detail. Therefore, there must be a reason for this curious ordering. John wants to call attention to Mary's presence at the banquet because she will play an important role in what transpires. Being the caring and observant person she is, Mary notices that the wine has run out. Instead of taking matters into her own human hands, she does something much more effective. Approaching her divine Son, Mary informs him of the problem: "They have no wine" (John 2:3).

She offers no suggestions, gives him no advice, she doesn't try to use motherly guilt or coerce him in any way. In fact, she doesn't even ask Jesus to do anything. Rather, she simply alerts him to the fact that there is a problem that could cause great embarrassment for the bride and groom. And how does Jesus react? By performing his first miracle and changing the water into wine, thus saving the day!

Could Jesus have performed this miracle without Mary's intercession? Sure. But he chose not to. The Blessed Mother played a critical role in this miraculous manifestation of the Lord's power, and she wants to do the same thing in our lives. While he was suffering and dying on the cross, Jesus gave his mother to the beloved disciple, John. It has always been the opinion of the Church that John represented each of us, thus making her our mother as well. When we consider the tremendous effort that it must have taken Jesus to utter these words, it's hard to disagree with the idea that this was a very significant act. It also seems inconceivable to reject Christ's gift!

Whether it's battling anxiety or helping us get closer to Christ, Mary is our *secret weapon*. She was given to us by our Savior as he suffered on the cross. Know that she is with you and is anxious to assist with your problems. Turn to her with all of your worries and concerns. Just as she did at Cana, Mary will go directly to Jesus and intercede on your behalf. Your heavenly mother will never let you down!

Hail Mary, full of grace. The Lord is with you. Blessed are you among women and blessed is the fruit of your womb, Jesus. Holy Mary, Mother of God, pray for us sinners, now and at the hour of our death. Amen.